BOUDICCA

ANCIENTS IN ACTION

Boudicca
Marguerite Johnson

Catullus
Amanda Hurley

Cleopatra
Susan Walker & Sally-Ann Ashton

Hannibal
Robert Garland

Horace
Philip Hills

Lucretius
John Godwin

Martial
Peter Howell

Ovid: love songs
Genevieve Liveley

Ovid: myth and metamorphosis
Sarah Brown

Pindar
Anne Pippin Burnett

Sappho
Marguerite Johnson

Spartacus
Theresa Urbainczyk

Tacitus
Rhiannon Ash

ANCIENTS IN ACTION

BOUDICCA

Marguerite Johnson

B L O O M S B U R Y
LONDON · NEW DELHI · NEW YORK · SYDNEY

Bloomsbury Academic

An imprint of Bloomsbury Publishing Plc

50 Bedford Square　　　1385 Broadway

London　　　　　　　　New York

WC1B 3DP　　　　　　　NY 10018

UK　　　　　　　　　　USA

www.bloomsbury.com

First published 2012

Reprinted 2013

British Library Cataloguing-in-Publication Data

A catalogue record for this book is available from the British Library.

ISBN: PB: 978-1-8539-9732-7

Library of Congress Cataloging-in-Publication Data

A catalog record for this book is available from the Library of Congress.

Typeset by Ray Davies

Contents

For Leni, Jack and Kate

Acknowledgements and Conventions

Thank you to my colleague and friend, Terry Ryan, for his insightful comments on the draft manuscript, and to Thom Fulton for his proofreading, suggestions and editorial advice. I am also indebted to Brian Bosworth who read and offered advice on the first chapter and to Leni Johnson for discussions on the last chapter.

Thank you also to Jane Holland and Salt Publishing for permitting the inclusion of the poems 'Not Exactly a Virgin,' 'Suicide,' and 'Headless Woman' from the collection *Boudicca & Co.* (Cambridge: Salt, 2006). Thank you also to Amanda Sebestyen who advised me on the inclusion of Catherine Arthur's artwork, 'Boudicca,' reproduced from her article, 'The Cancer Drawings of Catherine Arthur', *Feminist Review* 41 (1992): 27-36. Banksy is also gratefully acknowledged for providing the image of the Boudicca Clamp (would that all art truly belonged to the people as his does). For the photograph of Boudicca and her daughters in the tee-shirt, thank you to Cancer Research UK's Race for Life, especially Jo Sefton for arranging the copyright. For the photograph 'Boudicca agrees, DEEDS NOT WORDS', thank you Tim Dalinian and the wonder that is copyleft. Use of George Gale's caricature, published in the *Daily Telegraph* on 11 June 1987, was smoothly arranged by Dawn O'Driscoll from the Telegraph Media Group Limited.

Finally, I am grateful to The University of Newcastle for study leave during the summer and autumn of 2010, which provided the time to undertake this project, and to Deborah Blake for her careful and patient editing.

*

All translations, unless otherwise indicated, are my own. Translations of Dio are based on the Greek text by Earnest Cary (1924; Cambridge, Massachusetts: Harvard University Press, 1982); translations of Tacitus' *Annals* are based on the Latin text by John Jackson (1937; Cambridge, Massachusetts: Harvard University Press, 1969). Translations of the *Histories* by Tacitus are based on Charles Dennis Fisher's text (Oxford: Clarendon Press, 1911). For the *Agricola*, I consulted R.M. Ogilvie and M. Winterbottom's edition (Oxford: Oxford University Press, 1975).

Tacitus spells Boudicca's name as 'Boudicca' and Dio spells it 'Boudouika' (rendered as 'Buduica' by Cary). Throughout this book, I have adopted Tacitus' spelling unless I am referring to specific and notable variations such as those found in works of late antiquity (as in Chapter 4).

Some of the references contained in the Notes are not included in the Select Bibliography as they deal with specific matters not directly pertaining to Boudicca. The Select Bibliography lists works on Boudicca and Roman Britain. References in the text are to authors and the relevant page numbers of their work, with the complete references appearing in the Select Bibliography.

Abbreviations

Agr. = *Agricola* (Tacitus)
Ann. = *Annals* (Tacitus)
BG = *De Bello Gallico*, or *On the Gallic War* (Julius Caesar)
Claud. = *Life of Claudius* (Suetonius)
Ep. = *Epitome* of Dio

Geog. = Geography (Strabo)
Hist. = *Histories* (Tacitus)
Il. = *Iliad* (Homer)
Suet. = Suetonius
Tac. = Tacitus

Roman Britain tribal/place names and modern equivalents

Atrebates: Territory = Hampshire, West Sussex and Surrey

Brigantes Territory = Northern England and a substantial part of the Midlands

Camulodunum: Colchester, centre of the territory of the Trinovantes

Catuvellauni: Territory = Northern bank of the Thames and northwards to Hertfordshire

Corieltauvi (also known as the Coritani): Territory = East Midlands; Lincolnshire, Leicestershire, Nottinghamshire, Derbyshire and Northamptonshire

Deceangli: Territory = North-east Wales

Dobunni : Territory = North Somerset, Bristol and Gloucestershire

Iceni: Territory = Norfolk

Isurium: Aldborough

Londinium: London

Manduessedum: Mancetter

Mona: Anglesey

Ordovices: Territory = North-western Wales

Silures: Territory = South Wales

Trinovantes: Territory = North side of the Thames estuary in Essex and Suffolk, also encompassed territory now located in Greater London

Verulamium: St Albans

11

Watling Street: Track that extends, east to west, across Britain

Individuals: British

Antedios: leader of the Iceni at the time of Claudius' invasion; died *c.* AD 47; succeeded by Prasutagus

Boudicca: wife of Prasutagus, leader of the Iceni rebels in AD 60-61

Calgacus: Caledonian leader who fought the Roman army of Agricola at the Battle of Mons Graupius in *c.* AD 83/84

Caratacus: along with his brother, Togodumnus, was the heir to the Catuvellauni territories; waged guerrilla warfare against the Romans for some nine years

Cartimandua: leader of the Brigantes, a tribe whose territory was located in northern England, with its capital at Isurium (Aldborough); played a key role in the capture of Caratacus

Cassivellaunus: leader of both the Catuvellauni and the Trinovantes; entered into treaties with Rome in 54 BC

Prasutagus: leader of the Iceni, husband of Boudicca

Verica: deposed chieftain of the Atrebates, a man recognised in Rome as *rex*; it was his pleas to Claudius to reinstate him, having been ousted by Caratacus and Togodumnus, which instigated the invasion of AD 43

Venutius: husband of Cartimandua; the queen divorced him and acquired for herself a consort, Vellocatus, his arms-bearer

Individuals: Roman

Agricola, Gnaeus Julius (AD 40-93): military tribune in Britain under Paulinus (AD 58-62) and its longest serving governor (AD 77-85); Tacitus' father-in-law and subject of his biography, *Agricola*

Agrippina (AD 15-59): fourth wife of Claudius, sister of Caligula and mother of Nero

Augustus (63 BC-AD 14): emperor (27 BC-AD 14)

Caesar, Gaius Julius (100-44 BC): general and statesman; invaded Britain twice: 55 and 54 BC

Caligula (AD 12-41): emperor (AD 37-41); disastrous attempt to invade Britain in AD 40

Cerialis, Petilius: commander of Legion IX; suffered serious defeat at Camulodunum but went on to face Boudicca's forces in what was to be the last battle she fought against the Romans

Claudius (10 BC-AD 54): emperor (AD 41-54); 'leader' of the invasion of Britain in AD 43

Decianus, Catus: procurator of Britain in AD 61; his rapacity is blamed for contributing to the rebellion of Boudicca; when she sacked Camulodunum, he fled to Gaul

Didius Gallus, Aulus: governor of Britain (AD 52-57)

Messalina (*c.* 12 BC-AD 48): third wife of Claudius and Nero's cousin

Nero (AD 37-68): emperor (AD 54-68); ruled during the rebellion of Boudicca

Ostorius Scapula, Publius: second governor of Britain (AD 47-52)

Paulinus, Gaius Suetonius: appointed governor of Britain in AD 58/59; in AD 61 he made an assault on the island of Mona (Angelsey); responsible for leading the Roman forces that ultimately defeated Boudicca

Plautius, Aulus: leader of the Legions sent to Britain by Claudius in AD 43; the first governor of Britain (AD 43-47)

Sabina the Elder, Poppaea: mother of Poppaea Sabina the Younger; she committed suicide in AD 47 as result of the machinations of Messalina

Sabina the Younger, Poppaea (AD 30-65): second wife of Nero

Tiberius (42 BC-AD 37): emperor (AD 14-37)

Introduction

Two major written accounts of Boudicca remain from antiquity: Tactitus' *Annals* Book 14, and the *Epitome* of Dio's *Roman History*, Book 62. The works of these two authors form the centrepiece of the methodology of this study, which focuses on the Latin and Greek texts, particularly the style, sentiments, vocabulary and multi-layered meanings contained therein. While additional background on the Boudicca uprising is needed for context (namely modern historical interpretations of the years AD 60-61, as well as the limited but ever-increasing archaeological records), the two ancient authors are of foremost importance because they present the uprising in terms of their own values, moralities and social structures (features of their writings that are of vital significance to a study of Boudicca).

While numerous works on Boudicca have been produced within the last half century, and particularly the last twenty years, most of these situate the writings of Tacitus and Dio within broader historical accounts of the uprising. Many of these works, be they historical or fictional, tend to utilise the ancient sources as supplements to specific aspects of the event. It is the intention herein to reverse this methodological order and to treat what we know of Boudicca and the Iceni first and foremost within the context of what Tacitus and Dio tell us. In this sense, the two central chapters of the book function as exercises in text analysis, which primarily aim to shed light on how the Romans reacted to the uprising as well as to demonstrate the various literary techniques and characteristics of both authors.

In this sense, I take my authorial and scholarly cue from Sandra R. Joshel who, discussing Tacitus' portrait of Messalina, states: 'I am concerned with the writing of history, not with history as a set of events'.[1] This approach takes into account the fact that historical writing in antiquity was not stable, meaning that it was not primarily motivated by an authorial drive to present facts alone. While facts exist, they are not the dominating characteristic of the texts, but employed (to the writer's best ability and, sometimes, by a process of selective inclusion or omission) to provide frameworks in which authors such as Tacitus and Dio can then expound upon more pressing concerns: religiosity, morality, issues of gender, political theories, patriotism and other matters of import.

It is the Boudicca of the Roman and Greek imaginations that interests me and who receives the most attention in this study. This is not to deny that there is a discernable order of events and a traceable timeline in the works of both Tacitus and Dio, to which archaeology has increasingly come to attest. Nor is it to refute the existence of an outstanding female leader of the Iceni who featured prominently in the events of AD 60-61. Instead, it is to acknowledge Boudicca within a historiographical context as a living, breathing reality as well as a literary entity created by the ingenious artistry of two major authors. Such an approach places her perfectly within the heroic struggle between the ultimate world power and a throng of recalcitrant anti-heroes who rise up from the pages of history to leave a remarkable and indelible impression on readers throughout the centuries and up to the present day.

*

Chapter 1 presents an historical overview of Roman-Britain from its earliest years to the rebellion of AD 61. This chapter also includes a brief account of Boudicca's people, the Iceni, introducing some information on their background and lifestyle (while their battle practices and aspects of their leadership systems are treated in Chapters 2 and 3).

This is followed by the centrepieces on Tacitus (Chapter 2) and Dio (Chapter 3), each divided into two sections better to facilitate discussions of what are intricate and complex pieces of writing. Tacitus, for example, creates characterisation largely through comparisons and contrasts between his protagonists and the minor individuals who comprise both the *Histories* and the *Annals*. Thus the second component of Chapter 2 demonstrates how his portrayal of Boudicca is constructed via a complex web of intratextual allusion within the *Annals* to create a cumulative image of the rebel leader patched together via association with other individuals both in Britain and Rome itself. It also explores how meaning is accumulated through intertextuality, as Tacitus – in the *Annals* – 'returns' to his earlier work, the *Histories*, to shed light on his rebel within a broader imperial context.

Similarly, in order to emphasise Dio's moral and ethical interpretation of the great figures of history, the second component of Chapter 3 presents an analysis of the manner in which he portrays the Roman general, Gaius Suetonius Paulinus. Not only does this serve to elucidate Dio's extensive use of Greek value terms to underscore his creation of a hero worthy of ancient epic, but also his tendency to evoke character – and, indeed history – through the use of extended speeches (a feature in keeping with Homeric and Vergilian epic as well as the historiographical style of Thucydides).

These two chapters offer different levels of interpretation; for students with developing skills in the area of ancient history or for the general reader who does not want too much detailed textual analysis (but rather an introduction to the ways in which the ancients wrote), the first part of both chapters may suffice. For those with more interest in the technicalities of ancient historical writings, the second part of both chapters offers an extended analysis of the nuances of the stylistic features of Tacitus and Dio.

The last chapter addresses the ongoing fascination with Boudicca and examines her later life (or, rather, lives) through the lens of Reception Studies. The legacy of Boudicca throughout the ages has begun to attract serious scholarly attention over the last decade, particularly the re-emergence of her presence in late antiquity through to the early modern European age and into the Victorian era. While this 'journey' of Boudicca – from late antiquity to the twenty-first century – is addressed in Chapter 4 in order to provide a sense of continuity from the portraits of Tacitus and Dio, it is the appropriation of Boudicca by women such as the Suffragettes and their later feminist successors, be they artists, poets or political campaigners, that is a particular focus.

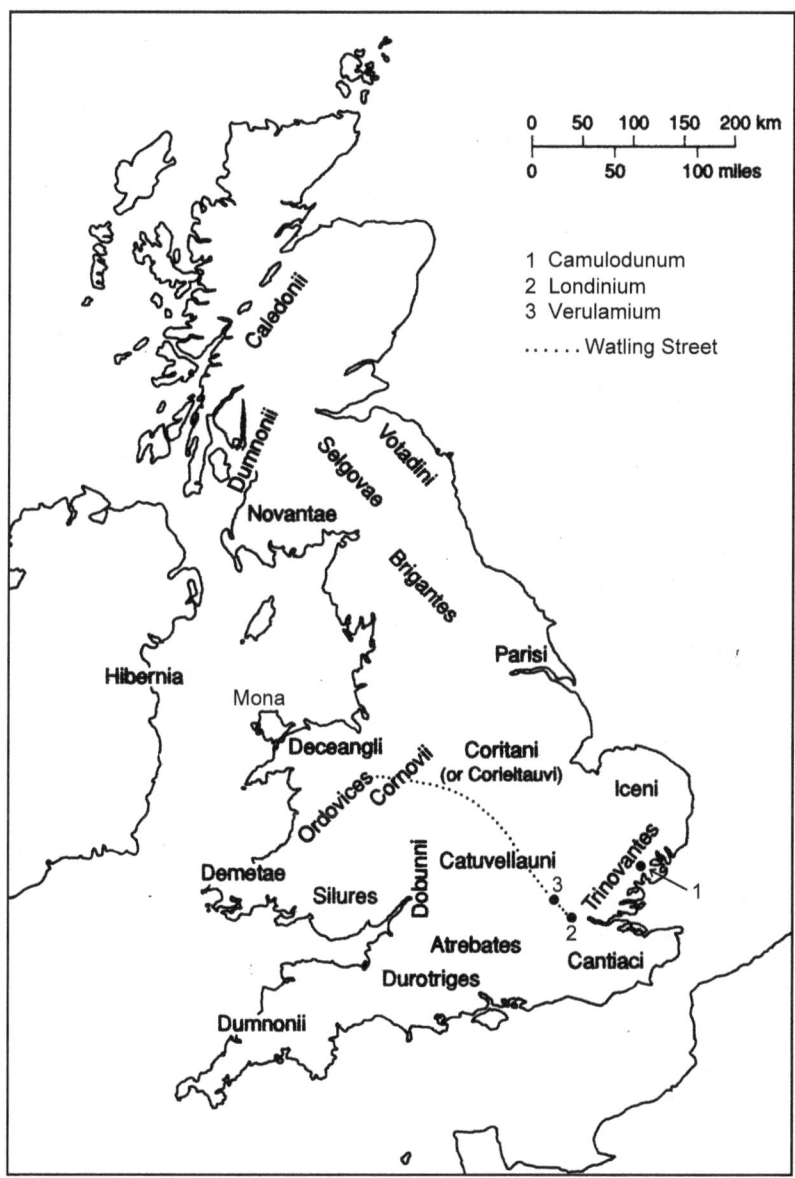

Roman Britain

1

Boudicca and the British Revolt Against Rome

For seventeen years, the Iceni had suffered at the hands of their supposed allies: their people had been taxed to pay for the costs of being invaded, the young men had been taken to serve in the foreign army, their rulers had been emasculated and their warriors had even been deprived of their weapons by a people who were meant to be their allies. Any dissent had been put down with brutal force but while the Romans could beat the Britons in battle, they failed to win their wholehearted support – and the Romans knew this only too well (Collingridge, 192).

Vanessa Collingridge's overview of Boudicca and her people, the Iceni, is an insightful and succinct representation of the situation in Britain when this powerful woman led a full-scale revolt against her oppressors, the Romans.

Boudicca's courage and her legacy have been the subjects of numerous books, both popular and scholarly, as well as films – from the silent production *Boadicea* (1928) starring Phyllis Neilson-Terry, to the television film *Boudica* (2003) starring Alex Kingston. There are also many portraits and other artistic representations, the most famous being Thomas Thornycroft's bronze statue which stands next to Westminster Bridge and the Houses of Parliament in London (erected in 1902). As well as being a symbol of the oppressed, the colonised and the dehumanised, she has become the feminine embodiment of insurgency and free-spiritedness. She is the 'Other', the barbarian, the individual who would submit to no invader no matter what the consequences – and the consequences were dire.

We have little by way of accurate or stable historical information on Boudicca. There are no written records from the Britons themselves, but we do have two accounts from those on the side of the victors: Tacitus (AD 56-117) and Dio Cassius (*c.* AD 150-235). Of these, only Dio furnishes an impression of what Boudicca may have looked like, and his portrait is an *ideal* that suits an *idea*; to him she is the stereotypical wild woman of the Celtic netherworld. Her body is *megiste*, usually rendered 'tall' in most English versions, and testimony to the formulaic nature of Greek and Latin descriptions of the peoples of Britain and Northern Europe – generically referred to as Celts and/or Gauls[1] – that inevitably paint them as being of impressive height.[2] She is also described as possessing a 'terrifying gaze' and a 'rough voice', and wears the mandatory torc. We have no idea whether this is an accurate portrait or not. We do know, however, that this representation by Dio reflects the Greek and Roman fascination with physiognomies, particularly when it came to peoples categorised as decidedly *un-Greek* or *un-Roman*. These people were categorised in part according to the Greek and Roman tendency to 'read' the body and, as individuals and cultures, they rarely escaped being 'read' the wrong way. As a 'typical British Celt', therefore, Boudicca possessed a large frame that equated with her large appetite for aggression; thus she is one of Callimachus' Titans,[3] a remnant of a past race still thought to thrive at the ends of the known world.

David Rankin explains (1995: 22): 'Likening Celts to Titans was happily in tune with the deeply rooted Greek mythopoeic custom of assimilating the terrifying and the unknown to Greek notions of a prehistoric past.' The comparison to giants, this emphasis on the sheer physical strength of the Celtic peoples, is also a significant means of indirectly explaining – somewhat defensively – why they were so successful against the civilisations of the Mediterranean for so many centuries. As reflected on numerous occasions in Homer's *Iliad*, a true hero proves himself by combating his equal; facing numerous men of lesser strength and skill is all very well, but defeating a man of equivalent standing makes the victory all the more honourable. Thinking thus in terms of the ancients, the imperial army truly met its match in the tall, powerful tribes of the Iceni and their ilk, and the difficulties in subduing them becomes, most importantly in the minds of the Romans, explicable. As P.C.N. Stewart writes on Julius Caesar's commentary on the Britons: 'the enemy may be uncivilized, but they are not so far inferior that their defeat is a mean achievement – quite the opposite' (3).

An historical overview of the Roman invasions

Julius Caesar and the invasions of 55 and 54 BC

The challenge presented to the imperial forces of Rome to conquer Britain began in 55 BC with the first campaign of Caesar, which followed and coincided with three years of operations predominantly against the Gallic tribes, whom Caesar claimed had received support from their British counterparts (*BG* 4.20). After previously engaging in a show of force against the Germans by crossing the Rhine, in August 55 BC Caesar and two legions crossed the Channel and somewhere along the coast of Dover they encountered the Britons for the first time. As the campaign was not successful in terms of achieving any significant impact on the land or its people, another incursion on a much larger scale was planned for the following year. In his account of the second campaign, Caesar admits that the Britons' style of fighting proved difficult for the Romans to counter successfully: the heavy armour of the soldiers and the strategic positioning and tightly organised movement of the standards meant they were unable to engage with the erratic foe and their guerrilla tactics (*BG* 5.16).

Neither campaign saw any significant extension of the empire, as Tacitus summarises so deftly:

> ... it was the Divine Julius who, first of all Romans, entered Britain with an army; though he successfully caused dread among the inhabitants and took possession of the coast, it can be discerned that he revealed it, not bequeathed it (*Agr.* 13).

Likewise, Strabo writes:

> The Deified Caesar crossed over to the island twice, although he came back in haste, without accomplishing anything great or proceeding far into the island ... (*Geog.* 4.5).[4]

As a counterweight to these two views, however, is the treatment by Dio Cassius, which stresses the glory won by Caesar for the venture and the opportunities he had opened up for future exploitation of the island (*Hist.* 39.53). Caesar had demonstrated to the Senate and the Roman people, as Tacitus obliquely states, that Britain was ripe for the taking. Although the foray of 55 BC was limited to the south-east of the island, it was favourably received in Rome with a thanksgiving of twenty days (*BG* 4.37.5). That of 54 BC resulted in treaties with Cassivellaunus, most likely the leader of both the Catuvellauni (a tribe north of the Thames) and the Trinovantes (a tribe whose territories were predominantly concentrated in Essex and bordered those of the Catuvellauni). The conditions of surrender involved legal and procedural terms, 'which specifically indicate the first steps in forming a province out of conquered territory' (Frere, 27). Once these measures were in place, however, the Romans exhibited no interest in further expeditions for the best part of a century.

1. Boudicca and the British Revolt Against Rome

The age of Augustus (27 BC-AD 14) and Tiberius (AD 14-37)

During the reign of Augustus there was a policy of good-will or shrewd political machination that was decidedly non-military in nature between Rome and the peoples of Britain. While Dio suggests otherwise (*Hist.* 49.38.2; 53.22.5; 53.25.2), indicating that Augustus did in fact plan military incursions into Britain owing to unrest in certain regions, Strabo presents a consistent historical account that attests to peaceful relations, including a much-quoted passage describing the dedications on the part of various British chieftains on the Capitol, as well as embassies and paying court (*Geog.* 4.5.3), all of which suggest a ratification of treaties already in place between certain tribes and the emperor.[5] Indeed, Augustus himself, in *Res Gestae* 32, lists the names of two British kings who came as *supplices* (i.e. refugees) to Rome.[6]

Such clear cases of peaceful relations, however, do not necessarily mean that the Britons as a 'whole' were on politically friendly terms with Rome; a reality that would not have been lost on Augustus, as R.G. Collingwood and J.N.L. Myres state: 'He can hardly have been blind to the fact that across the Channel a strong state was growing up, progressive in its civilization and by no means friendly to Rome in its spirit: a state whence no overtures of friendship were forthcoming, except from its exiles' (74).

Augustus' policy certainly had benefits for the Roman economy with profitable import and export duties and as Tiberius followed his predecessor's diplomacy, invasion remained off the agenda for, essentially, a hundred years.

Caligula (AD 37-41)

As far as Caligula's policy concerning the island stands, there is a discrepancy between ancient and modern opinions, as well as between modern scholars themselves. It is clear that there was an attempt at invasion in AD 40, although there are divergent reasons provided as to its motivation.[7] What is a common feature of ancient writing on the subject, and an example of the difference between it and modern interpretations, is the story of Caligula's orders to his men, assembled somewhere along the Gallic side of the Channel, most likely near Boulogne, to collect seashells as the spoils of war (Suet. *Caligula* 46; Dio 59.25). Both Suetonius and Dio present the event as an example of the emperor's eccentric and erratic behaviour. In contrast, Rankin suggests that 'it might have been a calculated assertion of power over the sea, and by inference, what lies beyond the sea' (1996: 57). David Braund extends Rankin's line of argument, suggesting that Caligula was not insane (in this instance) but performing a salutary ritual extolling his triumph over Oceanus, god of the seas:

> The invasion of Britain had long been seen to require the conquest of Ocean. Evidently, the hostile tradition of Gaius' [Caligula's] British campaign has developed from a literal interpretation of the metaphor (found in religious belief) which was a standard feature of the discourse of conquest at the periphery, especially in Britain. No doubt Gaius did indeed present his British campaign as the conquest of Ocean (95).

Claudius (AD 41-54)

It was not until the reign of Claudius that the conquest of Britain was fully launched and successfully executed. The campaign began in AD 43 when Claudius mounted an invasion ostensibly to 'reinstate' Verica,[8] the deposed chieftain of the Atrebates and a man recognised in Rome as *rex*. It was the movements of Caratacus and his brother Togodumnus, heirs to the Catuvellauni territories, into the territory of the Atrebates, which gave Verica cause to appeal to Rome. This request for assistance was no doubt interpreted by the emperor and his advisors as a matter evidencing political unrest in southern Britain (Braund, 97). Claudius ordered an army of four legions – II Augusta, IX Hispana, XIV Gemina and XX Valeria – plus auxiliary troops, totalling approximately 40,000 men, led by Aulus Plautius (who was to become the first governor of Britannia), with commanders including Titus Flavius Vespasian (the future emperor) and Gaius Geta. The forces amassed, following orders from Claudius, attest to his ambitions in relation to Britain; Braund rightly suggests that, Verica aside, '[Claudius] needed a striking military success to confirm his imperial stature. Moreover, an invasion of Britain retained much of the aura of daring and exoticism that it had had in the time of Julius Caesar' (97).

Despite the difficulties in the crossing and subsequent landing of his forces, Plautius successfully overcame the initial resistance to the extent that he stabilised control over the south-eastern corner of Britain as far as the Thames. Upon these successes, Claudius came to the island in person and assumed command, and it is recorded that he graciously received approximately eleven chieftains who surrendered to him. Dio (*Ep.* 60.21-2) credits Claudius with leading the campaign that resulted in the capture of the Trinovantes centre, Camulodunum, 'the main target for the first campaign' (Aldhouse-Green, 40) and a place that was to play an important role in the rebellion led by Boudicca.

The time Claudius spent in Britain earned from the Senate the title 'Britannicus' in addition to other accolades, including a triumph and the institution of an annual festival (Dio 60.22; 23). Two commemorative arches were also erected, one in Boulogne, his departure point, the other in Rome. What remains of the inscription on the Roman arch reads: '[Claudius] subdued eleven kings of Britain without any reverse and received their surrender and was the first to bring barbarian nations beyond the ocean under Roman sway' (Potter, 9). Coins were also minted in his honour, inscribed with the triumphal formula *De Britannis* (concerning the Britons) and depicting him either on horseback or driving a four-horse chariot.[9] Despite these initial successes of AD 43, however, Caratacus continued to wage guerrilla warfare for the remainder of that year, and indeed for the next eight years.

From AD 43 to 47 the Romans concentrated their efforts in lowland Britain, expanding their power into the East and West Midlands under the command of Plautius. Tribes that cooperated were rewarded with Roman recognition of their independence albeit on a client-based status. This diplomatic technique of exercising control was most likely the means by which the Romans won over Antedios, leader of the Iceni at the time of Claudius' invasion, thereby securing peaceful relations between the tribe and the occupying force.[10] However, late in AD 47 the Iceni became embroiled in an uprising against the Romans, instigated by Publius Ostorius Scapula, who had replaced Plautius as governor. At this stage in the history of the occupation (as noted above), the south and east of Britain had been secured, and alliances were being established with tribes outside the areas controlled by Rome. Less secure regions not yet won over by the Romans, however, were still a problem, and with the appointment of Ostorius late in the year when winter had already set in, certain recalcitrant tribes rose up, acting on a naive assumption that Ostorius would not initiate immediate reprisals. They were wrong. In order to secure the province prior to full-scale military operations westward, Ostorius disarmed all the British peoples east of the Trent and the Severn (*Ann.* 12.31), including the Iceni.

Tacitus describes the Iceni at this point in history as 'a powerful tribe, not weakened by war' who, having initially and willingly 'joined the alliance' became 'the first to resist' the forced disarmament (*Ann.* 12.31). To this warrior culture, this act of imperial domination 'was the height of emasculation, especially when it was probably rudely enforced by detailed searches of farms and fields' (Collingridge, 135). The Iceni accordingly summoned neighbouring tribes to join them in the uprising but, despite choosing ground favourable to themselves, were quickly vanquished by Ostorius with only a few cohorts; their defeat pacified 'those who were wavering between war and peace' (*Ann.* 12.31-2). Ostorius then campaigned against the Deceangli (of north-east Wales) and others beyond the Trent-Severn line, culminating in the suppression of the Silures at the mouth of the Severn. A legionary camp was established in their territory and at the same time, to allow legionary forces to be relocated on the new frontier, Ostorius established a *colonia* at Camulodunum in the heartland of the Trinovantes (*Ann.* 12.32). The subsequent guerrilla warfare involving remnants of the Silures and others including the Ordovices to their north was ostensibly led by Caratacus, lasting through to AD 51.

Following the defeat of the Iceni, Antedios disappears from history. In the light of Ostorius' handling of a rebellion by the Brigantes immediately afterwards, by executing a handful of those who instigated hostilities while pardoning the tribe as a whole (*Ann.* 12.32), it is most likely that Antedios was held responsible for the Iceni uprising. As a result the Romans installed Prasutagus, husband of Boudicca, as a more reliable and loyal tribal leader.

By the time of Caratacus' capture in AD 51, the occupying forces had control of not only the eastern and south-eastern tribes, including the Iceni, Trinovantes and Catuvellauni, but had extended west, north and north-west, subsuming the territories of the Dobunni, the Corieltauvi, Deceangli and neighbouring peoples of north-east Wales. They also made significant progress throughout the Midlands, controlling the territory of the Brigantes and the loyalty of their female ruler, Cartimandua, the mastermind of the trap that finally snared Caratacus.

The province remained relatively stable following the death of

Ostorius in AD 52 and the ensuing governorship of Aulus Didius Gallus, who consolidated existing gains from AD 52 until the one year governorship of his replacement, Quintus Veranius in AD 57/58 (*Ag.* 14). He in turn was replaced in AD 58/59 by Suetonius Paulinus who, according to Tacitus, had two successful years as governor, consolidating gains and reducing other tribes (*Ag.* 14).

The age of Boudicca

The governorship of Paulinus was an appointment described by Guy de la Bédoyère as 'probably the most decisive in the history of Roman Britain' (36). During the first two years of his appointment, Paulinus concentrated on quelling tribal outbreaks and establishing garrisons (*Ag.* 14). And, after significant success in these endeavours, he turned his focus to Mona (Anglesey), the island off the north-west coast of Wales, perceived by him at this stage of Roman occupation (AD 61) as the bastion of British resistance to Rome, essentially because it was a major centre of Druidism.

For the Romans, the Druids had been a source of intrigue and fear, an image reflected in Caesar's account (*BG* 6.13-14). The emperors exercised varying degrees of prohibition concerning them or, more expressly, their religion. During the reign of Augustus, for example, Roman citizens were banned from involvement in Druidism (Suet. *Claud.* 25); it was also outlawed during the reigns of Tiberius and Claudius (Pliny *Natural History* 30; Suet. *Claud.* 25). The ancient sources tend to focus on the Roman association of Druidism and human sacrifice as the major reason for the rejection of the religion and its leaders; nevertheless, the power and influence the Druids exerted over the Britons, combined with their anti-Roman stance, are the more obvious reasons for imperial policy concerning them.[11]

Paulinus' attack on Mona entailed striking at the most significant centre of Druidic power in Britain. In AD 61 (or AD 60) men from

Legions XIV and XX and auxiliaries most likely moved through the territory of the Deceangli and then ventured across the Straits of Menai to Mona. Tacitus (*Ann.* 14.30) describes the event in spectacularly dramatic terms. Facing the Romans on arrival was a mass of men and women standing on the shoreline; while the women rampaged in long, dark robes, with streaming hair, brandishing torches, the Druids cursed the legionaries. Nevertheless, the Romans overwhelmed these otherworldly forces. Tacitus, with an eye for depicting the common-sense and utilitarian attitude of the very worldly Romans, goes on to describe the aftermath of the encounter: the establishment of a garrison (probably at Segontium on the mainland) and the destruction of the Druids' sacred groves on Mona (*Ann.* 14.30).

During the course of the conclusion of the campaign at Mona, Paulinus was suddenly confronted with a revolt of the Iceni, an event described by Malcolm Todd as 'next to the Batavian revolt a decade later, the most serious rebellion against Roman rule in any province during the early Principate' (70). As noted previously, the Iceni under Antedios had risen against Rome in AD 47, slighted by the demand that they disarm. Roman reprisals are not evidenced in any of the sources. The emergence of Prasutagus as the new king led to the re-establishment of stable relations between the tribe and the Roman administration for almost a decade and a half. Prasutagus, however, died at this point in time, bequeathing the kingdom to his two daughters and the emperor, Nero.

If Prasutagus had thought that his compliance (*obsequium*, Tac. *Ann.* 14.31.1) with the Roman imperial machinery would secure fidelity and honour in return, he was very much mistaken. His wife Boudicca was flogged, his daughters raped and the estates of the nobles ransacked. These outrages are usually regarded as the principal trigger for the outbreak of hostilities by the Iceni and their allies at the time of Paulinus' campaign at Mona. Tacitus explains these humiliations (*Ann.* 14.31) not as causes of the war *per se* but as a

31

component part of an overall series of acts meted out to the Britons by a tyrannical foreign superpower. The hatred the British rebels harboured towards the Romans is also explained by impositions such as the temple of 'the deified Claudius', which Tacitus describes as a constant reminder of 'eternal tyranny' (*Ann.* 14.31). The construction of this temple at Camulodunum began after the death of Claudius in AD 54 and was a reminder to the Trinovantes of their displacement and disenfranchisement. The structure, even by Roman standards, was excessive (Sealey, 20) and its exorbitant costs were extracted from the leaders of the allied tribes.

What Tacitus achieves through a narrative structured by these cumulative accounts of oppression is a complex collective of right-eous grievances against the Romans on the part of the Britons, especially the Iceni, which culminates in the treatment of Boudicca and her daughters. In contrast, Dio, a less nuanced historian and writer, does not build such an intricate historical background with foundations of layered narrative and long-standing grievances; in-stead, he summarises the cause of the rebellion as monetary in nature. The procurator of the island, Catus Decianus, demanded repayment of monies interpreted (perhaps not incorrectly) by the Britons as a gift from Claudius. Seneca the Younger also required payment in full of his (unambiguous) loan of some 40,000,000 sesterces (*Ep.* 62.2).

Both historians provide a vivid account of Boudicca's subsequent ravenous destruction of specific Romano-British sites. The first tar-get of the rebels' attack was Camulodunum, which occurred while Paulinus was engaged at Mona. The *colonia* was utterly destroyed, with massive loss of life. Paulinus set out on horseback at once to Londinium, heading down Watling Street,[12] only to abandon the centre and its people upon learning of the scale of the disaster and the size of the forces being assembled under the leadership of Boudicca. He set out to rejoin his army, already on the march, stopping briefly at Verulamium, and decided it too could not be saved. Boudicca's forces descended on Londinium and its hapless inhabitants, and followed up with an assault on Verulamium, which also resulted in the utter destruction of the centre and those who had remained.

Paulinus' response was to face the rebels in a pitched battle and to choose a location that would effectively counter their guerrilla tactics and the effectiveness of their superior numbers. While the exact site of this battle is unknown, scholars tend to favour Manduessedum (Mancetter). Paul R. Sealey, for example, puts forward several persuasive reasons:

> ... one may assume that as the Roman army pressed south-east on its march from Angelsey, the Britons made their way up Watling Street into the Midlands towards the approaching Romans. Paulinus is unlikely perhaps to have strayed far from Watling Street itself and the scene of the final encounter may be sought somewhere along the route. A case can be made for Mancetter in Warwickshire, where high ground approaches the road to give a terrain that fits the meagre topographical sketch of the battlefield in Tacitus (40).

The centres attacked by the forces led by Boudicca were not traditional British settlements but communities established by the Romans. As already noted, Camulodunum was created as the first *colonia* in Britain, established in AD 47 as part of Ostorius' strategic move to cement control of the province from the estuary of the Thames to that of the Severn in anticipation of an attack by and against the forces mustered by Caratacus. As a *colonia*, which saw the Trinovantes 'driven from their lands and treated as captives and slaves' (Sealey, 17), it became a settlement of Roman citizens, retired legionaries, with full legal rights. Londinium, according to Tacitus, was a settlement 'that was not distinguished by the title of "colony", but was exceedingly frequented by many merchants and traders' (*Ann.* 14.33).

Finally, Verulamium was a *municipium* (the only one in Britain), a tribal centre that received special favour under the imperial regime of Rome[13] but was lower in status to a *colonia*, and hence the occupants were not given the rank of citizen although they may have enjoyed many of the same privileges.

The first point of attack by Boudicca's forces, primarily comprised of the Iceni and Trinovantes, was Camulodunum. As news of the impending onslaught reached the inhabitants, they realised that the *colonia* desperately needed more Roman troops as there was only a meagre garrison *in situ*. Appeals were made to Decianus, who accordingly sent two hundred men (*Ann.* 14.32), but this was nowhere near adequate to protect the people who took refuge in the temple precinct and were inevitably slaughtered. The wholesale destruction of Camulodunum is attested by the archaeological evidence, notably by what is termed the 'Boudiccan destruction horizon', a layer or horizon of debris, including building fragments, red soot, daub and molten glass, which can be as thin as a few centimetres to as thick as a metre (Sealey, 22).

Londinium and Verulamium met the same fate as Camulodunum. M.J. Trow notes (2003: 175) that Paulinus, along with a small cavalry unit, reached 'the ramshackle collection of huts that was Londinium' before Boudicca, reminding the reader of Antonia Fraser's explanation for the delay of the British rebels, namely that they were too busy with drunkenness and debauchery. As discussed in Chapter 2, Tacitus explains that Paulinus assessed the situation in Londinium and decided to abandon the settlement in order to focus on the protection of the island overall, 'determined to save the country as a whole at the expense of one town' (*Ann.* 14.33). His description of the situation is characterised by pathos and vivid evocation:

The lamentation and the tears of the pleading inhabitants could not make him turn back; he issued the signal for departure and accepted into the march those capable of following. Those unfit for war because of their sex or wearied by age or detained by attachment to the site, were left to the enemy (*Ann.* 14.33).

Tacitus goes on to state that Paulinus adopted the same attitude towards Verulamium. He claims that the forces of Boudicca chose such sites because they promised plunder and little exertion. The end result was that approximately 70,000 'Roman citizens and allies fell' (*Ann.* 14.33), which looks like exaggeration (to make the achievement of putting the rebellion down seem all the more formidable). Tacitus mentions that they took no prisoners; Dio elaborates with 'unspeakable slaughter. Nothing that was not in itself dreadful was meted out to the captured peoples by them' (*Ep.* 62.7).

In regard to the 'Boudiccan destruction horizon' at Londinium, Collingridge writes that it 'is almost as evident here as it is in Colchester [Camulodunum] but it appears to be more patchy and less intense' (236). She goes on to explain, however, that the horizon of debris still points to a temperature of around 1000 degrees Celsius. Similar evidence has been found at Verulamium, with the 'horizon' extending beyond the settlement by approximately five kilometres. The devastation of these three settlements was extensive, ruthless and efficient. Boudicca certainly received immense recompense for the humiliation of herself and her daughters.

The Iceni

In Roman times, the territory of the Iceni included Norfolk and part of Suffolk; to their west were the Corieltauvi, to the south, the Trinovantes and Catuvellauni (coinage from both territories has been found on Iceni land). During migrations in the sixth century BC from Belgium and Holland across the North Sea, northwest Europeans established communities along the Norfolk rivers and marshes with peaceful integration of the indigenous population (Webster, 46). They were followed approximately fifty years later by people from the Marne Valley, described by Graham Webster as 'aristocratic warriors, looking for territories with people to conquer and rule (47). The main settlement of the tribe in the late Iron Age and early Roman-Britain era was at Venta Icenorum (Caistor St Edmund), to the south of the modern city of Norwich. Venta, discovered in 1929, was most likely established or laid out in the latter part of the first century BC with a street grid covering some 20 hectares (50 acres). The Romans most likely heard of the tribe for the first time during the campaign of Caesar in 54 BC, 'when', as D.F. Allen writes, 'after he had decided to take the Trinobantes into protection, five other tribes sent deputations of submission to him'. Allen further specu-lates that although the Iceni are not named at the time of the invasion of Claudius in AD 43, 'they could well be among the eleven unnamed kingdoms whose submission he recorded in the inscription on his triumphal arch at Rome' (1).

As previously discussed, by the time of the invasion of Claudius, the main component of the tribe was ruled by Antedios, although as John Wacher has noted, there appear to have been at least three discrete provincial organisations within the kingdom. Wacher further states that the Iceni overall appear to have been somewhat isolated as only a small number of their coins 'from the pre-conquest period travelled outside the Norfolk region' (243). Likewise, their lack of contact with peoples outside Britain is attested via excavations, as Richard Hingley and Christina Unwin note:

> Imported objects in pre-conquest contexts are relatively rare and, although a coin tradition did develop in this period, the evidence suggests that the tribal aristocracy did not adopt Roman ways of drinking, feasting and dressing. In fact, traditional hand-made pottery

appears to have remained common across much of the territory into the early first century AD and possibly in some cases until AD 60 to 61 (33).

Their conclusion is that the Iceni were a conservative people compared to some of the other tribes of south-eastern Britain, although archaeologist John Davies now questions just how isolated the Iceni were, noting that 'The Iceni did not receive the same range of imports from the Mediterranean world as did sites further south, where there is evidence for imported pottery and amphorae. However, archaeology is now showing that Norfolk was engaged in significant trade, both with the continent and with other parts of Britain' (Davies, 127).

Despite the accounts of Tacitus and Dio that attest to the ferocity of the Iceni as warriors – accounts that we should not necessarily dismiss – the Iceni were also farmers; they planted crops and raised animals and thus possessed one marker of civilisation as defined by the Romans. Indeed, it is now known that farming had been established throughout Britain since the Neolithic age, and there is little evidence to suggest that the Romans improved the agricultural practices that had been developed in Britain, as Barry C. Burnham has argued: 'As far as farming techniques are concerned ... the Roman impact is very difficult to disentangle from broader trends spanning the later first millennium BC and the early first millennium AD' (129). Basing his own work on the extensive analysis of agriculture in Britain by M. Jones, Burnham acknowledges that the former 'could identify no specific innovations in crop production in the half-century or so following the invasion, while the iron-age staple crops continued to predominate with few, if any, significant new introductions'.[14]

In addition to the practice of agriculture, the Britons possessed advanced proficiency in craftsmanship and artistry. When considering this in relation to the Iceni, the Snettisham Hoard provides compelling archaeological evidence for the sophistication of the tribes of the Norfolk region. Priceless artefacts, including the famous Marriage Torc or Snettisham Great Torc dating from *c.* 75 BC, have provided evidence of the high level of metal-working skills of the people from the Iceni region. The Marriage Torc, made of electrum (three parts gold to two parts silver) is 20 cm (7.9 inches) in diameter and is shaped by the twining of eight wires, coiled into delicate ropes, adorned with stylised terminals. Additionally, the volume of treasures unearthed in the region of East Anglia – similar to if not as striking as the Marriage Torc – also attests to the prosperity of the Iceni and the relative peace that prevailed in their region during the first century BC – financial and social factors necessary for the production of sophisticated material culture. As well as more than a hundred other torcs, there have been hoards of additional jewellery pieces as well as precious metal coins and also pottery from the region of East Anglia.[15] Miranda Aldhouse-Green has commented on the noticeable wealth of the Iceni, evident in their impressive gold artefacts and the fortunes of Prasutagus, which she ascribes to 'the production and sale of salt, a valuable commodity in the European Iron Age and Roman periods' (26). The sheer wealth of the region, and particularly of the royal and noble families, puts into sharp perspective the actions of the Romans upon the death of Prasutagus.

2

Tacitus' Account

Publius (or Gaius) Cornelius Tacitus (AD 56-117) was a senator who rose to the Consulship in AD 97 and later held an extensive provincial governorship in Asia. He is best known as *the* major historian of the early Roman empire. Like Dio after him, Tacitus' work consistently shows a concerted effort 'to come to grips with the rule of a single man, and an interest in a more antiquarian history, concerned with a distant and glorious past' (Marincola, 30). As such, Tacitus writes primarily for the senatorial class and is cognisant of the self-imposed need to incorporate both the glorious and inglorious contributions of individual men in the events that constitute Roman history. He is a moralist, a particular exponent of the value of *virtus* (manly gallantry) and *libertas* (freedom; the right of a free man to be involved in public affairs), who is thus drawn to recording not only the history of the wider imperial arena, encompassing Britain and beyond, but also the internal machinery of the Roman court (particularly in the *Annals*). Be it describing and analysing events abroad or internal, Tacitus is attentive to exploring actions and individuals through the lens of the precept that history should inspire good deeds and discourage evil ones (*Ann.* 3.65). In this sense, he takes his historiographical cue (in part) from Livy (59 BC-AD 17), who endeavoured in his own writing to use moral *exempla* as a means of not only recording events but warning his readers of the opprobrium likely to be incurred through indulgence in vice and corruption (see Preface 10, *History of Rome*).

Tacitus' *Annals* 14.29-39 and *Agricola* 14-16 constitute the earliest, most extensive extant sources on the rebellion lead by Boudicca. The historian's knowledge of Britain comes from various sources, two of whom he names in *Agricola* 10.3 when discussing the geography of Britain: 'The shape of the entirety of Britain has been compared by Livy and Fabius Rusticus, the most eloquent (*eloquentissimi*) of ancient and modern authorities, to an oblong shield or battle-axe.' Rusticus, a contemporary of Claudius and Nero, is not an author whose works have survived. Sources indicate, however, that he was hostile to Nero and a supporter of Seneca, one of his patrons, and a man in direct financial contact with Britain at the time of the rising hostilities against Rome. Rusticus is regarded as a major source on the later years of Nero's reign and no doubt Tacitus consulted his work for Boudicca.

Additional accounts of the uprising were most likely supplied by Pliny the Elder and perhaps by Cluvius Rufus, both of whom are mentioned by Tacitus.[1] A noted historian, Rufus was a contemporary of Rusticus, and, like him, his historical work is no longer extant. In the *Histories* 1.8.2, Tacitus tells us that Rufus was governor in Spain; he praises his skill in the arts of peace-time (*vir facundus … pacis artibus*) but notes he was lacking (*inexpertus*) in war-time experience. While it is obviously difficult to establish echoes of Rufus' words in Tacitus' writing – except when the latter explicitly mentions him (as in *Ann.* 14.2 on the high-jinks at court between Agrippina and Nero), as his work covered the age of Caligula down to AD 70 – it would be unusual if Tacitus did not familiarise himself with the history and incorporate some of its information and features into his own account of the uprising. However, scholars such as E.W. Black and G.B. Townend caution against a conclusion that argues for extensive use of Rufus by Tacitus largely because of the perceptions of the latter's fondness for rhetorical flourish and hyperbole. There is also Tacitus' own reference to Rufus' inexperience in military matters. Nevertheless, one should not be too dogmatic in concluding that

Tacitus did not use Rufus just because they had wildly divergent approaches; indeed, Tacitus not only explicitly mentions Rufus, but also goes to the extent of praising his *style*, suggesting that he did read him and use him as a source (see Trow 1964). In relation to Pliny the Elder (AD 23-79), Tacitus cites the author at *Annals* 13.20, 15.53 and *Histories* 3.29. Pliny's *History of Rome*, written in thirty-one books, and his twenty-volume work entitled the *German Wars* (neither of which has survived) were no doubt utilised by Tacitus for his *Germania.*[2] Additionally, Pliny's interest in Britain, as revealed in the extant work, *Natural History*, would suggest it, too, was consulted by Tacitus.

The *Annals* begins with the death of Augustus in AD 14 and the reign of Tiberius, and thus heralds the certainty of imperial permanence and the political focus on dynastic inheritance. By its very thematic nature, therefore, the *Annals* is concerned with intrigues at court and other matters in the capital, and while its author is sometimes accused of being too obsessed with affairs at Rome, his treatment of major incidents within the empire and its burgeoning frontiers, such as the rebellion of Boudicca, reveals an undeniable interest in matters external to the city, which are in turn conveyed in a style that is both compelling and exhilarating. Beginning and ending with the reigns of Tiberius and Nero respectively, the work deals with events that began some forty-two years before his birth and ended when he was twelve years old. This makes it likely that Tacitus accessed other oral accounts of the events in Britain in AD 60-61 in addition to those provided by his father-in-law, Gnaeus Julius Agricola, who was a military tribune there between AD 58-62. As a senior officer serving under Paulinus, he almost certainly had first-hand experience fighting against Boudicca.

When it comes to speeches, Tacitus exhibited literary licence and convention in the tradition of all major historians from antiquity (cf. Miller, also Levene). The speech of Boudicca, for example, is most likely pure invention, although she may have given some form of oratorical inspiration to her forces prior to the battles she led. Just as Dio would later do with his native Greek, Tacitus has the leader of the Britons speak in Latin, something that Eric Adler finds useful in ascertaining the high degree of artificiality of the speech she allegedly delivered:

> In addition, Boudica would not have addressed her troops in either Latin or Greek; as a result, it is highly unlikely that Tacitus and Dio acquired adequate information on her speeches' contents. Finally, Tacitus and Dio offer such disparate versions of Boudica's harangue that it seems far-fetched to believe that either historian intended to present an accurate account of an actual speech (178).

The modern historian or literary critic must pay particular attention to the actual words placed in Boudicca's mouth and analyse them in terms of the level of authorial voice or intent conveyed therein. One must also be alert to the poetic and rhetorical nature of ancient historiography for, in covering the years between AD 14 and 96, Tacitus is employing the literary skills of the poet and orator, combining the stylistic features of both and paying careful attention to evoking just the right amount of emotional response in the reader.

Boudicca's rebellion

In the *Annals*, Tacitus provides background to the uprising of the Britons, which sets the scene for military intervention on the part of the Romans. Following a concise overview of the activities in Britain prior to the leadership of Paulinus (*Ann.* 14.29), Tacitus begins his narrative with a spectacular description of the commander at Mona, where the Druid bastion was being assailed. Here the British rebels function in the account as a thematic precursor to the role Boudicca goes on to play in the *Annals*. Without an explanation of the specific causes of the Mona campaign, Tacitus briefly depicts Paulinus and his men crossing over to the isle from the mainland (*Ann.* 14.29.3-4), abbreviating the account in order to hasten the spectacle that awaits the Romans (and the reader):

> Standing on the shore was the opposing line: a mass of arms and men, with women moving in-between in the manner of the Furies in funereal robes, with streaming hair, carrying torches; while a circle of Druids poured out ill-omened curses and raised their hands to the sky. The strangeness of the sight struck the troops as though their limbs were suspended, and they offered their immoveable bodies to wounds. Then with the encouragements of their leader and inciting each other lest they fear a womanly and fanatic band, they brought to bear the standards against the enemy so as to meet and cut them down, enveloping them in their own flames (*Ann.* 14.30.1-2).

Tacitus' picture of the indigenous forces at Mona embodies a powerful image of the women of Britain *per se* as well as the awesome presence of the Druids. The Britons amassed at Mona are *active* participants: the women move between (*intercursare*) the dense collective, their hair streams down (*deicere*) and they brandish (*praeferre*) torches; simultaneously, the Druids raise (*tollere*) their hands and pour out (*fundere*) curses. In contrast, the Romans are initially rendered *inactive*: the spectacle causes them to stop as if suspended or frozen (*haerere*) and their bodies are immobile (*immobile corpus*), thus rendering them vulnerable to wounding. It takes the initiative of their leader Paulinus – Tacitus' hero – to rouse them into action. Rankin suggests that the women at Mona, clad in black, 'could be representatives of the raven-black goddesses who move among the warriors in battle spreading dismay with their curses' (1996: 269), an interpretation providing a specifically British – or, more generically, British-Celtic – context for the vision that so confounded the Romans.

The raven in British-Celtic folklore was a powerful animal totem: 'A raven sits on the shoulder of the terrifying Medb [mythological Irish queen] and ravens roost on the dying Cu Chulain [Irish hero]' (Rankin 1996: 269). An interpretation that associates the women at Mona with such mystical, religious and animal totemism is possibly reinforced by Pomponius Mela's description of the isle of Sena (Île de Sein), off the coast of Brittany:

> Sena in the British sea opposite the Ofismician Coast [the English Channel], is notable for an oracle of a Gallic deity who is tended to by priestesses, perpetual virgins, nine in number. They are called *Gallicenae* and are thought to be gifted with a singular ability to stir up the seas and winds with incantations, and to transform themselves into animals if they wish, to heal those regarded by others as incurable, to know the future and to provide predictions – but only for navigators who set forth in order to consult them (*De Situ Orbis* 3.6).

Peter Berresford Ellis regards these women as akin to female Druids, writing that the '*Gallicenae* certainly have the attributes of Druidesses as depicted in insular Celtic literature where they had become "sorceresses" and "wizards" ' (98). The role of the Druids as intermediaries between mortals and gods is evident in the passage by Mela, where the priestesses not only tend the deity but are privileged with divine powers such as shape-shifting and control of the elements, both attributes of witches, not only in Celtic mythology but Greek and Latin literature also. The influence of the Druid class on kings and warriors is also shared by the *Gallicenae* as evidenced in the advice provided to sailors.

The overt exoticism of the Britons, epitomised by the description of the women at Mona and reflected in the accounts of Mela, is also emphasised in the next action ascribed to Paulinus:

> After this a garrison was imposed on the conquered peoples and the

sacred groves consecrated to savage superstitions demolished: for they regarded it divine law to sprinkle altars with captive blood and to consult the gods with the entrails of humans (*Ann*. 14.30.3).

The connection Tacitus makes between Druidism and human sacrifice is also mentioned by Caesar (*BG* 6.16.1-5) – although his account of such rites is accompanied by an explanation as to why they were performed, namely to propitiate the gods. While the Romans themselves practised human sacrifice on several noted occasions (but certainly not regularly), a senatorial decree in 97 BC had expressly forbidden it, and by the late republic the Romans regarded it as a ritual practice that distinguished them from those they perceived as barbarian, be they the Gauls (including the Britons), the Jews or the Christians.[3] The Roman destruction of the sacred groves is explicitly embedded in the connection made between them and human sacrifice: the altars in the groves are bathed in *human* blood and the gods are contacted via *human* entrails. Yet despite the Roman abhorrence of these practices, which they would have regarded as impious according to their own perspective, there was possibly a more utilitarian reason for destroying the sites of British cult. Collingridge has argued that Druid power-bases such as Anglesey 'had the power to influence tribal leaders and mobilise the masses to rise up in revolt' (177). She goes on to discuss the possibility that 'it was the Druids of Anglesey who had given both credence and support to Caratacus' guerrilla army that became the scourge of the Romans in the years after the Claudian conquest until his capture in AD 51' (177). If this were the case, such political and military power needed to be quashed, and the destruction of sacred groves and other spiritual locales was a symbolic attack not only on the Druids and their influence, but on the British gods per se and thus the morale of the people. As John Creighton emphasises: 'Whilst the rape of Boudicca's daughters and calling-in of loans have been the traditional explanations for the rebellion, this final violation of the sacred groves must have shaken some deep-rooted sentiments as well' (300).

Tacitus proceeds from the destruction of the groves to the next challenge faced by Paulinus, namely the revolt of Boudicca (*Ann.* 14.30). The overview he puts forth is not only concise, but objective and unembellished:

> The king of the Iceni, Prasutagus, renowned for long prosperity, named Caesar as heir along with his two daughters, having thought such compliance would keep injury away from his kingdom and house. It resulted in the contrary, to the extent that his kingdom was laid to waste by centurions, his household by slaves, as if captured in war. At the same time, firstly his wife Boudicca was subject to lashings and his daughters violated with dishonourable acts (*stuprum*): the principal men of the Iceni were stripped of ancestral estates and the relatives of the king treated as purchased slaves (*Ann.* 14.31.1-3).

The theme that emerges here is one of freedom versus slavery, which is emphasised in the speech of Boudicca later recorded by Dio. The sudden change in the fortune of the Iceni, from prosperity, autonomy and dignity to enslavement and humiliation, is signposted as the cause of the ensuing uprising; indeed it is the hatred felt by the Iceni towards the Roman veterans that is emphasised by Tacitus (*Ann.* 14.31.4-5).

On the subject of Prasutagus' will, Tacitus offers no rationale for the omission of Boudicca as one of the beneficiaries. One could speculate, however, that Prasutagus may well have distrusted his wife because he suspected or had verification of her anti-Roman sentiments. This possibility certainly fits the narrative as Tacitus presents it; the singling out, for example, of Boudicca and her daughters for public humiliations of the worst kind, may not only be testimony to imperial ferocity, but also a very open and drastic response to a

woman who had been known to despise the Romans. Christoph M.
Bulst suggests this motivation on the part of Prasutagus, and also
speculates that 'his choice was probably to some extent influenced by
the advice of the Romans, since his own position as king was far from
one of independence' (498).

The hatred that ignites among the Iceni signals disaster for the
Romans, a portentous event that is heralded by a series of omens:

> Meanwhile, for no clear reason the statue of Victory at Camulodunum
> fell, the back turned as if retreating from the enemy. The women in
> their madness were cavorting, screaming destruction was at hand and
> strange noises were heard from the senate-house; the theatre re-
> sounded with lamentations and a vision of the ruined colony was seen
> in the estuary of the Thames: at this very time the Ocean looked
> stained with blood, the ebbing tide left the likeness of human corpses,
> interpreted by the Britons as hope, by the veterans as a threat (*Ann.*
> 14.32.1-2).

Tacitus' treatment of divine signs is somewhat different in interpretation from the corresponding passage in Dio. Whereas the latter
refers to the omens as 'an early warning concerning the catastrophe'
(*Ep.* 62.1.1), the former suggests that they portend disaster for the
Romans and that is all – there is no concept of the gods being on the
side of the Romans and thereby warning them via the signs; indeed
the Britons are the ones who interpret these phenomena in a fortui-
tous light.

Dio mentions more or less the same omens as Tacitus but omits
one major incident: the tumbling statue of Victory at Camulodunum,
the site of the *colonia* established by Ostorius in AD 47 for his
veterans. As Aldhouse-Green notes (181), a falling Roman statue in
a restless colony is a significant and symbolic event, albeit one that is

virtually impossible to verify. C.J. Simpson, however, argues vehemently in favour of literary invention on the part of Tacitus:

> ... whatever may be the plausibility of an actual Statue of Victory at Camulodunum, it is most likely that Tacitus' report is not based on any reality at the Roman colony but has its foundations elsewhere as literary invention. It is a literary topos not a recollection of reality that has been served up to Tacitus' educated readers in Rome (386).[4]

Tacitus is following a long-standing historiographical tradition that includes the use of recorded omens preceding major events. Yet Simpson omits reference to the cultural significance of such alleged happenings, the stories of such portentous events that coloured the oral traditions of the ancients and gave meaning to important historical episodes via divine and phenomenological motifs. In this sense, the story of the falling statue of Victory at Camulodunum is as vital a Roman cultural signifier – be it recorded in writing or passed down orally – as Livy's preservation of the stories accompanying the first Gallic invasion of Rome in the early fourth century BC.

After the concise summation of the background of the uprising at *Annals* 14.31, which refers to the treatment of Boudicca and her daughters following the death of Prasutagus, Tacitus takes his time before reintroducing her into the narrative. His interest in the mechanics of both Roman and British movements prior to the military encounters, and in the activities of the Roman forces prior to Paulinus' decision regarding the pitched battle, occupy three chapters, thereby delaying – textually-speaking – the reappearance of Boudicca. In contrast to Dio's account of the rebellion in Britain and his portrait of Boudicca, Tacitus' version situates Boudicca within the larger tactical frame of the British uprising and the Roman response. The result is less emphasis on Boudicca in the narrative of Tacitus compared to her starring role in the drama of Dio.

2. Tacitus' Account

After the ominous incident concerning the statue of Victory, Tacitus describes the fate of the inhabitants at Camulodunum (*Ann.* 14.32). Despite Roman attempts to fend off the rebels, initiated by the procurator Decianus, consisting of a hastily compiled group of some two hundred men 'without proper weapons' (*Ann.* 14.32.3), Tacitus gives the impression that they simply could not cope with the suddenness and sheer ferocity of the uprising. The historian keeps the role of Decianus to a minimum, allowing the action to speak for itself as to the effectiveness – or lack thereof – of his leadership.[5] On the subject of the treatment of the female and aged residents of Camulodunum, for example, Tacitus (*Ann.* 14.32.4) may be seen to imply a carelessness on the part of the Romans resulting in the defenceless quickly being surrounded by a horde of barbarians (*multitudo barbarorum*). He continues:

> And, in fact, the rest was plundered or set aflame in the assault: the temple, in which the soldiers themselves crowded withheld for two days and was then captured (*Ann.* 14.32.5).

Worse still, when relief arrived in the form of Legion IX, commanded by Petilius Cerialis, they were annihilated by the Britons. The latter escaped with what remained of his men while the much-derided Decianus fled to Gaul.

Dio's version of the encounters with the Britons is decidedly unclear compared to what we read here in Tacitus; he notes the absence of Paulinus – who was still engaged in the aftermath of Mona – and names this as the reason for the rebels' success in taking 'two Roman cities' (*Ep.* 62.7.1), presumably meaning Camulodunum and Londinium (the latter being the town to which Tacitus proceeds to turn his attention). Despite the vagueness, Dio acknowledges the presence of Boudicca in the two sieges prior to her final encounter with Paulinus (*Ep.* 62.7) and emphasises her leadership in the destruc-

49

tion of Camulodunum and Londinium by prefacing the events with a character portrait of her and a lengthy war oration delivered before the rebel forces (*Ep.* 62.3-5; 62.6.2-5). As such, it is only by reading Dio in conjunction with Tacitus that we understand implicitly that Boudicca not only provided motivation for the sack of Camulodunum and Londinium, but was also a key participant.

As mentioned above, Dio alludes to two locations that fell to the Britons, whereas Tacitus specifies three: Camulodunum, Londinium and Verulamium. Tacitus recounts that Paulinus marched from Mona to Londinium, a location soon to be under attack by the rebels (*Ann.* 14.33.1). As testimony to his strategic leadership and military experience – which Tacitus contrasts to the haphazard impetuosity of Decianus – he left the centre to the Britons and set his sights on saving Britannia at the expense of the people of Londinium. He left the people of Verulamium to the same fate (*Ann.* 14.33.4). The brutality of the forces of Boudicca at these locales is testified in Tacitus' overview of the three sieges:

> It has been agreed that close to 70,000 citizens and allies fell in the previously mentioned places. Indeed, they neither took captives nor prisoners for sale nor other forms of war commerce, but they hastened with massacres, gallows, fires, crosses, as if punitive retaliation [*supplicium*] would inevitably return, but only after revenge has been snatched in the interim (*Ann.* 14.33.5-6).

This narrative, while indicative of the unequivocal effectiveness of the Britons' ferocity, lacks the explicit and disturbing detail found in Dio's account (*Ep.* 62.7.2-3). It is nevertheless testimony not only to the Britons' desire for vengeance but also to their fatalistic resolution to cause as much brutality before their own inevitable destruction. And with the arrival of Paulinus, the destruction of the Britons does indeed come, and following the description of the fall of the three communities, Tacitus turns his attention to the preparations of their Roman nemesis (*Ann.* 14.34). Tacitus (like Dio) is vague as to the whereabouts of the final encounter. While this was possibly Mancetter (as discussed previously), Aldhouse-Green has also suggested Paulerspury in Northamptonshire (196).

Tacitus' battle details in Chapters 34 and 37 of Book 14 frame the orations of Boudicca and Paulinus, recorded indirectly in contrast to Dio's use of direct speech. In Chapter 34, he summarises the strategy of Paulinus, namely to engage in pitched combat. He provides a description of the area and the placement of the Roman forces, their position accessible only via a narrow pass, with a wood behind them and an unobstructed plain in front (*Ann.* 14.34.2). The location ensured that there was no means by which the forces could be ambushed by the Britons and that there was only one field on which combat could ensue. He ordered his legionaries into 'serried ranks' flanked by light-armed troops with the cavalry on the extreme wings (*Ann.* 14.34.3). The careful, closely positioned organisation of the forces was designed to exploit the limited manpower available to Paulinus, who led 'approximately 10,000 armed men' in contrast to the superior numbers at Boudicca's disposal, which Tacitus describes only as multitudinous (*Ann.* 14.34.4). By contrast, his picture of the Britons describes them, unsurprisingly, as uncontrolled and lacking any specific strategic organisation; this combined with the emphasis Tacitus places on their overweening confidence (*Ann.* 14.34.4) and the placement of women in wagons to bolster their endeavour – thus making it difficult for them to move freely and retreat when needed – essentially explains their defeat.

Tacitus then turns his attention to Boudicca and provides a record, in the third-person, of her speech to her troops:

> Boudicca, riding in a chariot with her daughters before her, as she approached each tribe, proclaimed that it was customary for the

Britons to be led to war by women [*feminarum ductus*], but that on this occasion it was not as one born from a great ancestry avenging royal authority and power, but as one of the people [*vulgus*] having been deprived of her liberty [*libertas*], her body marked by lashings, the chastity [*pudicitia*] of her daughters stolen. The lusts [*cupidines*] of the Romans had progressed so far that neither bodies [*corpora*], nor age itself, nor virginity remained unstained [*impolluta*]. Nevertheless, at present were the gods of just revenge: a legion that had dared battle had fallen; the rest were hiding in the camps or were looking around for an escape. Certainly they will never endure the din and clamour of so many thousands, less still their onslaught and manpower; if they themselves weighed up the abundance of troops and the causes of the war, on that field they must conquer or fall. That was the resolve of a woman [*mulier*]: the men might go on living and acting as slaves (*Ann.* 14.35.1-5).

Her words, brief compared to the first-person harangue in Dio, present a woman who avows a genuine reason for her vengeful uprising; while the Romans prided themselves on waging war that was just and pious,[6] this 'barbarian' is shown as the one party with moral imperative behind her actions. Boudicca's high standing in the tribe of the Iceni and her status within that community as a free woman occupies a central tenet of her speech. She emphasises her reduction, and that of her daughters, to slave status by the actions of the Romans: she was flogged as any slave could be, and her daughters raped, as any slaves could be. This reversal of her status and that of her children emphasises their humiliation in a very public way – in front of the people over whom Boudicca 'ruled' – the Iceni. Thus Tacitus shows the barbarity of the Romans themselves in this instance, violating their own moral codes pertaining to warfare.

The depravity of the Roman forces under the imperial reign of Nero is symbolised in the speech of Boudicca through the emphasis on the body – her own marked body, and the bodies of her daughters.

The act of flogging literally marks Boudicca's body with the stigma of slavery, with the cultural sign of servitude, and thereby extols the virility of her Roman oppressors. The physical abuse endured by her daughters likewise reduces their humanity; the act of breaking their hymens is a signifier of Roman machismo at its imperial worst. The act is one of negation for it violently breaks something – a membrane to be precise – that can never be healed; like the scarring of their mother's body, the daughters of Boudicca carry the physical reminders of Roman savagery and power with them for the rest of their lives. Of course the scarring of the young women is not as physically prominent as their mother's; nevertheless they are, at the very least, as socially marred as she – more so, in fact – for they are rendered useless as women. Previously free young noble women highly prized as future wives and mothers, they are not only despoiled, but remain a constant reminder to the indigenes of Roman might, a power that may well have contaminated the wombs of the young women with bastard Roman offspring.[7]

On the theme of 'just and pious war,' Tacitus notes the initial success of the rebels, having Boudicca refer to 'the gods of just revenge' (*Ann.* 14.35.3) presiding over their early accomplishments. Here, as Aldhouse-Green suggests, Boudicca alludes to the failure of 'Cerialis' relief force from Legion IX and is probably also making scornful allusion to the cowardice she reads into the non-appearance of Legion II from Exeter' (194). These victories are short-lived, however, a fated reality Tacitus foreshadows by the introduction of Paulinus and his oration, which immediately follows that of his enemy. In this speech, which Tacitus describes as 'a combination of exhortations and entreaties' (*Ann.* 14.36.1), the script turns once more to the disarray of Boudicca's forces: '... more women than soldiers met the eye. Unwarlike and without weapons they would break immediately when they recognised again and again the steel and the courage of their conquerors – having learned from so many defeats' (*Ann.* 14.36.1-2).

The standard Roman view of the Celts, including the Britons, as undisciplined and disorganised fighters, is evident here. By implication, Tacitus shares the common view that such unstable and unpredictable people are not fit for self-determination. Indeed, much of the Roman vituperation against the Britons, and the Celtic people as a stereotypical whole, is encapsulated in this speech. Paulinus actually begins his oration with reference to the awful sounds made by the warring Britons (*Ann.* 14.36.1). His speech continues with a reiteration – under his command – of the key strategy outlined in *Annals* 34: they are to keep their order close (*Ann.* 14.36.4), which exploits the soldiers' familiarity with fighting together, each relying not only on himself but his fellow comrades. He then advises them to hurl one of their two javelins:

> … this would produce a deadly volley of fire that could travel about 100 feet (30 metres), and would have the further effect that the soft iron shafts bent on impact, so that if they struck in warriors' shields, they could not be pulled out and thrown back (Aldhouse-Green, 199).

This would render the shields useless and thus would begin the Roman onslaught of close hand-to-hand fighting, the Romans utilising short swords and shields with more efficiency than the long weaponry of the Britons, which was difficult to manoeuvre in a confined mêlée. Further, Paulinus forbade his men from pillaging amid the fighting; instructing them to pile up the corpses and remain patient for the plunder that would inevitably come (*Ann.* 14.36.4).

Tacitus' following chapter outlines the legionaries' exact implementation of Paulinus' orders, painting a picture of Roman military perfection:

> At first the legion, with a firm position, was motionless, and, holding

back to the narrow section of the field for defence purposes, ex-
hausted the enemy as soon as they approached closer with javelins
thrown with precision, and dashed forward in a wedge-like formation.
At the same time was the auxiliary attack; and the cavalry with lances
extended, broke through any obstinate or strong men (*Ann.* 14.37.1-
2).

Tacitus summarises the fate of the rest of the British forces: they
attempted flight, but this proved difficult owing to their own arrogant
placement of wagons full of supporters, which crowded the battlefield (*Ann.* 14.37.3). As John C. Overbeck writes: 'The wagons are
used with gruesome effectiveness: they are casually introduced in
chapter 34 as part of the holiday atmosphere, and now, in chapter 37,
they prove to be a death trap for the Britons' (136). And, as the
Romans begin their post-battle clean-up, no one is spared:

> The soldiers showed no remorse in the slaughter of the women, and
> even the baggage animals were speared and their bodies added to the
> pile of corpses (*Ann.* 14.37.4).

In a not-so-subtle juxtaposition of images, Tacitus refers to the
troublesome women in the same sentence as the baggage animals;
they are slaughtered indiscriminately and disposed of together, Tacitus' style matching the ruthless efficiency of the historical action he
describes. The last great battle is then summarised:

> The brilliance and the glory achieved on that day were equal to the
> victories of antiquity: for, it may be estimated that some 80,000
> Britons fell, some 400 [Roman] soldiers killed and not so many more
> wounded (*Ann.* 14.37.5).

While Tacitus has been impartial, almost sympathetic at times, his
bias comes to the fore in this passage: he begins the celebratory

sentence with the word *clara* (brilliance) and emphasises its meaning by following it, soon after, with *laus* (glory), the latter juxtaposed to *dies* (day) to expressly convey that it was this specific encounter, on this specific day, that heralded so much prestige for Rome. The sorry state of affairs pertaining to the Roman imperial forces and their lack of discipline (to say the very least) – as described by Tacitus in his depiction of the reaction following the death of Prasutagus (*Ann.* 14.31) – is hereby repaired by the comparison of the final encounter to the great military victories of Rome's forefathers.

Amid this jubilant passage and the description of the Roman clean-up operations, the Icenian leader is farewelled from the narrative in a single, simple sentence: 'Boudicca ended her life with poison …' (*Ann.* 14.37.6). Dio claims she died of an illness (*Ep.* 62.12.6) but makes no mention of any poison causing this, one possible interpretation being that she died from a wound resulting in infection. Tacitus' explanation, however, is more plausible as Boudicca would have been abundantly aware of the treatment that awaited her if she fell captive to the Romans. The treatment of Caratacus, captured in AD 51 and led through Rome in chains in the emperor's military triumph (albeit subsequently pardoned), would have left a strong impression on the Britons.

Tacitus spends the remainder of his narrative describing Paulinus as he completes the task of stamping out the rebellion and punishing the Britons. The commander spared no time nor wasted effort in clemency, even when it came to those merely suspected of insurgence. The tribes were punished with both fire and sword (*Ann.* 14.38.2).

This account in the *Annals* was preceded by a much shorter one in the *Agricola*. In the latter, Tacitus outlines a series of grievances on the part of the Britons (*Ag.* 15) and then makes a passing reference to Boudicca:

Having been incited one after the other by this and the like [anti-Roman sentiments], they all rose in arms, with a female leader, Boudicca, of royal blood (for they do not make distinctions pertaining to sex in military leadership) (*Ag.* 16.1).

There is no account of the battle or Boudicca's fate, yet the *Agricola* reminds the reader of one of Tacitus' key sources of information on the revolt: the subject of the text, Tacitus' father-in-law, Agricola, was military tribune in Britain under Paulinus and its longest serving governor (AD 77-85).

Boudicca and the bigger imperial picture

Boudicca and Cartimandua

A British contemporary of Boudicca was Cartimandua ('Sleek Pony'), leader of the Brigantes, a tribe whose territory was located in northern England, with its capital at Isurium (Aldborough). Cartimandua is discussed in some detail by Tacitus in both the *Annals* and the *Histories* and rightly so, for not only did she play a leading role in Romano-British politics of the first century BC, but her private life proved simply too scandalous to omit.

I.A. Richmond, in his treatment of the rule of Cartimandua, notes her significance in British and Roman history, a significance that he regards as being of more weight than the rebel Boudicca; that is until Boudicca burst onto the historical (and literary) stage as the outraged heroine and freedom fighter *par excellence*:

> ... until the moment when the neglectful terms of a husband's will and the tactlessness and bestiality of Roman officials drove Boudicca and her nobility into revolt, Cartimandua was in her own right much the more important figure and certainly counted for very much more in Roman eyes (43).

She was important to the Romans, as Richmond rightly observes, because she played a shrewd political game for the purposes of self-preservation and maintenance of power that suited Roman imperial policy in relation to the island.

In *Agricola* 17.1, Tacitus mentions that the inhabitants of the territory over which Cartimandua ruled were the most numerous in Britain; the region in question stretched from a substantial part of northern Britannia to the Midlands, which suggests a conglomeration of tribes. At the time of the Claudian invasion, the Brigantes were the most powerful tribe in Britain and at some stage under the rule of Cartimandua accepted their status as a client-kingdom. It is possible that she was already in power at the time of the invasion of AD 43, and she may well have been one of the eleven rulers who willingly surrendered to the emperor. Tacitus mentions her royal birth (*Hist.* 3.45.2) and as he does not go into the details of her ascendancy, one may assume that she had been queen prior to AD 51, the year in which she is first mentioned by the historian and called 'queen of the Brigantes' (*regina Brigantum* [*Ann.* 12.36.1]).

As the ruler of a massive territory, Cartimandua was by no means a monarch of a stable realm; the very nature of her kingdom meant that there were internal factions and her hold on power was not always secure. At *Annals* 12.32.3, Tacitus mentions tribal unrest among the Brigantes in AD 48 that caused Ostorius to return 'back from the brink of the Irish Sea' (Braund, 125). The episode is dealt with concisely by Tacitus: 'The Brigantes also, when a few who were initiating a call to arms were put down and a pardon offered to the rest, settled down quietly' (*Ann.*12.32.4). Cartimandua is not mentioned by Tacitus at this juncture but enters the narrative in relation to her role in the capture of Caratacus:

... [Caratacus] sought trust (*fides*) in Queen Cartimandua of the Brigantes, yet the defeated are entirely unsafe, and he was placed in chains and handed over to the victors nine years after the war in Britain began (*Ann.* 12.36.1).

After a series of major blows to the forces of Caratacus – culminating in the capture of his wife, his daughter and his brothers following the disaster of the battle at Abertanat in AD 51 where the Romans ended his insurgency once and for all – the rebel leader mistakenly put his trust (Tacitus uses the powerful word, *fides*) in Cartimandua and was betrayed. She handed him over to Ostorius. Her power play was deft, for as Sheppard Frere notes: 'If Caratacus succeeded, her rule was over' (64). Tacitus' use of *fides* in relation to the support Caratacus sought from Cartimandua, is therefore, deeply ironic; Cartimandua's *fides* was to Rome. As Braund writes: 'The reader is left to estimate her *fides* very low where British resistance is concerned, while excessive in regard to Rome' (127). Braund also makes the insightful observation concerning her presentation to the Romans of Caratacus in chains:

> ... the worth of Caratacus has been a feature of the preceding narrative, where he has been shown as a champion of prized *libertas* and an active leader of the British cause against *servitium* under Rome: the extended nature of that resistance is further indicated by Tacitus' observation that Caratacus had been handed over eight years after the invasion. By insulting such a man with bonds and handing him over to the Romans, the queen has shown her own *servitium* ... Although Cartimandua is Rome's friend, and Caratacus is Rome's enemy, Tacitus encourages the reader to admire the *libertas* of the latter and despise the *servitium* of the queen (127-8).

Following the capture of Caratacus, there was a renewed period of internal unrest, this time instigated by Cartimandua's husband, Venutius. In an attempt to distance herself from the anti-Roman Venutius, the queen divorced him and acquired for herself a consort, Velloca-

tus, the arms-bearer to her husband. Tacitus elaborates on her con-
niving tactics:

> But since the capture of Caratacus, Venutius from the Tribe of the
> Brigantes was [the one] outstanding in knowledge of military matters,
> as I have recounted above,[8] and long faithful and defended by Roman
> arms when he was married to Queen Cartimandua, soon – having
> been stirred up by the separation [from his wife] and forthwith by war
> – assumed hostilities even against us. But initially they struggled
> among themselves, and by shrewd artifices Cartimandua seized Venu-
> tius' brother and relatives. Thereafter her enemies were incensed,
> aroused with ignominy, lest they be subdued by the power [*imperium*]
> of a woman [*femina*], and with a strong and select army of young men,
> they invaded her kingdom. We foresaw this and despatched cohorts
> to undertake a fierce battle, which had an uncertain beginning but a
> positive end (*Ann.* 12.40.2-6).

This assessment of Venutius and, by comparison, Caratacus is somewhat surprising given that Tacitus is writing of men who declared
themselves the enemies of Rome. Both men are acclaimed for being
outstanding (*praecipuus*) in knowledge of military matters (*scientia rei
militaris*), although Tacitus ranks Caratacus ahead of Venutius. His
praise of the latter sets the tone for the passage on the turmoil in
Cartimandua's court and, more importantly, on Venutius' rebellion
against Rome. He is, like Caratacus, a rebel, an enemy of the empire,
yet Tacitus acknowledges his military skills and, prior to the rebellion,
his faithfulness (*fides*) to Rome, which had lasted for a long time (*diu*).
Tacitus' negative opinion on the rule of queens, revealed in *Germania*
45.9 ('the Sitones … are dominated by a woman and have degener-
ated not only from a state of freedom [*libertas*] but even from that of
servitude [*servitus*]'), for example, is apparent here in his description
of the effects of Cartimandua's tactics on her subjects. The latter,
ironically described as *hostes* (enemies), are incensed by her treachery,

which they interpret as humiliation at the hands of a woman. Tacitus interprets the event in gendered terms: Cartimandua's actions are not those of a leader – not even those of a queen – but of a *femina* (woman). On this most weighted term in Tacitus' rhetoric, Francesca Santoro L'hoir writes:

> The noun *femina*, used over one hundred times by Tacitus, connotes social and moral distinctions. While it can evoke sympathy, as when he laments the many *inlustres* [i.e. noble] *feminae* victimized by the Julio-Claudians, it can also convey opprobrium, as on the fifteen occasions when he couples it with words denoting legitimate male authority. The device is particularly effective in the *Annals*, where Tacitus uses it as a recurring component of innuendo (6).

Santoro L'hoir's comment on the juxtaposition of *femina* with words denoting masculine authority is exemplified in the above passage; Cartimandua's femaleness is seen as incongruous with her *imperium* (power), which is at the centre of her people's hostility toward her.

On Cartimandua's approach to *regnum*, Tacitus implies that it is her failure to rule her court, typified by her separation from her husband, and the unrest that results from this domestic turmoil – namely factional disputes – that inevitably contribute to the outbreak of open hostilities towards Rome. While Venutius is depicted with the adjective *praecipuus* and the quality of *fides*, which cause a tension in the account of his deeds (implying that they do not reflect his character), Cartimandua is defined by the phrase *callidae artes* (shrewd artifices), demonstrated by her seizure of Venutius' family members.

To a significant extent, Cartimandua is described in the *Annals* as a female despot. Not only does she fight unfairly, seizing her own subjects as hostages, she treats her people as slaves – sacrificing them in the process of serving her foreign master, Rome. Her frenetic style of leadership, fecund with autocratic manoeuvres, incites an internal

61

invasion of her own court by a select corps of young warriors. The passage in question possesses a latent sexual tone as the metaphorically emasculated men over whom she rules reassert their virility (note Tacitus describes them as strong young men); the use of the verb *invadere* (to invade, to enter, to seize), furthers this potent image.

The *Histories* provides an even more subjective, disdainful account of the queen in Tacitus' discussion of yet another domestic – hence tribal – uproar in the kingdom of the Brigantes, this time in AD 69:

> These discords and the repeated rumours of civil war spurred the spirit of the Britons via the encouragement of Venutius who, in addition to an innate ferocity and hatred of the name of Rome, was provoked by personal incentives concerning Queen Cartimandua. From a powerful noble lineage, Cartimandua ruled the Brigantes and had augmented her power after the capture, through deception, of King Caratacus, and was seen to have set in order the triumph of Claudius Caesar, from which followed wealth and luxury. With the separation from Venutius (who was her husband), she accepted in marriage and royal authority, his arms-bearer, Vellocatus. Immediately the household was in shock: for her husband, the support of the people; for the adulterer [Vellocatus], the wantonness and savagery of the queen. Therefore, Venutius called for armed support and at the same time, defection by the Brigantes themselves, forced Cartimandua to crisis point. At this time she petitioned the Romans for protection. Our cohorts and cavalry – from various battles – removed the queen from danger; the kingship was left to Venutius, the war to us (*Hist.* 3.45.1-4).

The portrait is hostile, to say the least, and Tacitus uses powerful vocabulary to condemn the queen. Amid her vast kingdom, Tacitus notes that there is *discordia* (discord) and the rumblings of *bellum civile* (civil war), which points to ineffectual leadership on Cartimandua's part. This interpretation is given even more credence when one considers the final sentence of the passage concerning the removal of the queen from her position and the appointment of the allegedly ferocious, anti-Roman Venutius. Indeed Tacitus provides some sense of empathy towards the latter, admitting that while he was to all intents and purposes a rebel, his actions were partially motivated by those of Cartimandua.

In addition to the use of a careful vocabulary on Tacitus' part, Cartimandua's characterisation is also shaped by the rhetorical method of narrating her story through her relations with men, namely Venutius, Caratacus and Vellocatus. As Tacitus displays an element of empathy in his discussion of Venutius, so he does in relation to Caratacus (*Ann.* 12.36) and both men – ostensibly enemies of Rome – emerge from the texts as anti-heroes at the very least, if not heroes proper. Indeed, it seems unbefitting for a leader who successfully evaded the Romans for some eight years, to be captured in the end by a *woman*, and an *unfaithful woman* at that, by means of *deception*. The reference in the above-quoted passage from the *Histories* seems to be deliberately concise in order to convey this sentiment: eight years of freedom is contrasted to essentially one day of capture by deception. The only one of the three who does not receive favourable treatment is, unsurprisingly, Vellocatus, the *adulter* (adulterer), who is shown to be under the queen's power; and in terms of her power, Tacitus outlines its dual nature: wantonness (*libido*) and savagery (*saevitia*). Thus, for Vellocatus – as well as Tacitus – Cartimandua's power is her seductive charm or, to put it more bluntly, her unbridled sexuality and the fear she can instil in others through her savage nature. Both are demonstrated not so much in relation to her new husband but in connection with Caratacus: her ability to seduce, to utilise her sensual nature – not necessarily in a sexual manner – combined with her propensity for cruelty, are made evident in her deception (*dolus, Hist.* 3.45), her false *fides* (*Ann.* 12.36) and her presentation to the Romans of the rebel in chains (*Ann.* 12.36).

While a ruler, Cartimandua is also a woman, and Tacitus inserts a clever conceit that marks this obvious connection by matching her disorderly kingdom with her fractured *domus* (household) in the *Histories* 3.45. Clearly this is not Tacitus' prejudice alone, for the Romans generally regarded queens – who were always foreign, hence marked by a double stigma – as unnatural, dangerous and immoral creatures. What is noteworthy in this context is the fact that the title *regina* (queen) is never used of Boudicca by Tacitus. In many ways, Tacitus' Boudicca bears more resemblance to Caratacus and Venutius than she does to Cartimandua. The traces of empathy that seep ever so faintly into the *Annals* during Tacitus' masterful discourse on the events of AD 60-61, are even more strongly felt when he returns to the narratives of Caratacus and Venutius later on. No such empathetic tone colours his portrait of Cartimandua.

Cartimandua, Messalina and Boudicca

The similarities between Cartimandua and Boudicaa are less pronounced than the differences, and as previously discussed, Tacitus is careful to draw his portraits of each of these barbarian women partially through the artistry of comparison, particularly contrast. Indeed Cartimandua is closer to Tacitus' Messalina, (*c.* 12 BC-AD 48), third wife of Claudius and Nero's cousin, than she is to his Boudicca who, as the following analysis demonstrates, seems to have been deliberately cast as a very separate if not superior example of the female of the species in Tacitus' drama of imperial Rome and Roman imperialism, standing – or rather, being placed – well ahead of the other two.

On the portrait of Messalina in Book 11 of the *Annals*, regarding the similarities with Cartimandua, Joshel's concise overview is an apt place to start (231):

Drawing on a commonplace of Roman moral rhetoric that associates uncontrolled female sexuality with chaos, Tacitus creates an adulterous wife whose desire creates disorder in the family, household, and social hierarchy ... .[9]

Echoes of Cartimandua's disorderly court and territory are thereby evident and illustrated in Tacitus' first reference to Messalina in the year AD 47,[10] which details her involvement in the accusations concerning Poppaea and Asiaticus:

> Messalina believed that Valerius Asiaticus, twice consul, was one of Poppaea's lovers and, while simultaneously gaping at the gardens, begun by Lucullus, which, Asiaticus was adorning with grace, she incited Silius to accuse both of them. Cajoled [into the conspiracy] was Sosibius, tutor of Britannicus, who through the appearance of good-will, was to warn Claudius to beware the power and wealth that threatened the principate (*Ann.* 11.1.1-2).

The background to Messalina's troublemaking was her dislike of Poppaea Sabina the Elder (mother of Poppaea Sabina the Younger, second wife of Nero) because she believed the woman had had relations with one of her own lovers, the ex-slave-cum-actor, Mnester (Joshel, 54), as well as her desire for Asiaticus' beautiful gardens.[11] Tacitus also mentions later in the *Annals* the incomparable beauty of Poppaea (*Ann.* 13.45.2), which may have also inflamed the jealousy of her antagonist. As the wife of an emperor now in his seventh year of office, Messalina's powers were at their height in AD 47, and she naturally, therefore, attended the interrogation of Asiaticus 'in the court (literally the 'bedroom') of the emperor' (*Ann.* 11.2.1). Thwarted by Claudius' sympathy towards the accused, Messalina endeavoured to manipulate matters by pressuring Lucius Vitellius (a successful politician during the reign of Claudius, and a favourite of the empress) to work on the situation while she embarked on the destruction of Poppaea.

Like Cartimandua, Messalina was a woman not to be thwarted, and Tacitus tells us that she hired men to harass Poppaea with threats of imprisonment in the hope of driving her to suicide. Asiaticus opened his veins, claiming that he would have preferred to have died via the machinations of Tiberius or the violence of Caligula rather than by womanly (*muliebris*) treachery (*fraus*) and the vicious (*impudicum*) mouth of Vitellius (*Ann.* 11.3.2). And at *Annals* 13.43.3 we are informed that Poppaea did in fact commit suicide.

Messalina later added to her portfolio of evil deeds by turning her attention to another lover:

> For she burned so for Gaius Silius, the most beautiful of young Romans, that she drove out of the marriage Junia Silana, a noble woman, in order that she could take possession of the vacancy and the lover. Silius was ignorant of his shamefulness and his danger: but if he had refused, destruction was certain, and he had hope of not falling, and at the same time advantages were great, so for solace he ignored the future and revelled in the present. That woman was not discreet but went to his house with many a retinue, cleaving to his steps, showering him with wealth and honours; afterwards, as if fortune was now transported, the slaves, the freedmen, belongings of the emperor were seen in the possession of the adulterer (*Ann.* 11.12.2-4).

Messalina inevitably grew weary of the simplicity of her adulterous manoeuvres and – motivated by a perverse desire for even more infamy – decided, on a whim, to accept Silius' offer of marriage (*Ann.* 11.26). Like Cartimandua, Messalina's affair threatened to fracture the court. An embarrassed but reluctant Claudius was forced to act, causing panic among the lovers. In the following vignette Tacitus creates a masterful evocation of imperial Rome gone mad as well as a remarkable example of intratexuality:

> Accordingly they separated, Messalina to the gardens of Lucullus, Silius, with anxiety disguised, to the duties of the forum. The rest scattered in varied directions with the advent of the centurions and their use of chains on those wherever they found them – be it on the streets or in hiding. ... In the meantime, with only three companions, she was suddenly alone and with the whole of the city having been traversed by foot, with a cart, which was used to remove the refuse of gardens, she entered along the road to Ostia with the sympathy of no one, so powerful the ugliness of her outrages (*Ann.* 11.32.2-3, 6).

As armed Rome comes to aid Cartimandua, armed Rome turns on Messalina; as Cartimandua facilitates Claudius' triumph, Messalina facilitates his humiliation. But in the passage above, the primary point of reference is not Cartimandua, but Boudicca, as Peter Keegan explains (111):

> Tacitus' representation of the ignominy of Messalina's journey and the extent of her social isolation stands against Boudica's portrayal prior to her final confrontation with Suetonius (*Ann.* 14.35). The Icenian queen rides on a chariot, not a compost wagon; she is accompanied by her daughters, not strangers; and Boudica is esteemed by her people, certainly not reviled.

Boudicca's barbarity is never in doubt, nevertheless she becomes the heroic anti-heroine, in contrast with the portrait of the 'sham Boudicca', Messalina. The echoes inherent between the two passages – *Annals* 11.32 (Messalina) and 14.35 (Boudicca) – are further reinforced by the rabble surrounding each woman: Messalina's hordes are far from heroes, fleeing her debauched love-nest, then making for the streets of the city or cowering in hiding places; Boudicca's men stand by her and bravely face the Roman onslaught while the women and children are positioned on the outskirts of the battlefield. In contrast, Messalina is ludicrously conveyed about in a refuse cart, a powerful pastiche of the war-chariot of Boudicca, fighting not for her damaged chastity or integrity, but manoeuvring – literally and figuratively – for the means of salvaging her self-inflicted ignominy.

Cartimandua, Agrippina and Boudicca

In Tacitus' final speech attributed to Caratacus, the captured rebel is in Rome, fighting for his life. In attendance is Agrippina (AD 15-59) – the new wife of Claudius, sister of Caligula and with Gnaeus Domitius Ahenobarbus, the progenitor of Nero. As she sits, listens and watches, he delivers an oration that reiterates the creed so regularly invoked by the Britons in their campaigns against Rome:

'Had my moderation in success been as great as my nobility and good fortune, I would have entered this city an ally rather than a captive; nor would you refuse to accept under a treaty of peace a man who rose from illustrious ancestors, ruling many tribes. My present lot is as hideous to me as it is magnificent to you. I possessed horses, men, arms and wealth; what wonder that I parted with them unwillingly. If you choose to rule over everything, must everyone accept slavery [*servitus*]? If I had been delivered immediately as a hostage, neither my fate nor your glory would have become famous: oblivion would have followed my supplication. But if you keep me unharmed, I will be an everlasting testimony to your clemency.' At this, Caesar bestowed his grace upon him, his wife and his brothers. Discharged from these chains, they also venerated Agrippina, who was sitting close by, conspicuous on another platform, with the same praiseworthy gratitude as the emperor. It was strange for a woman to preside before the Roman standards, it being new and without the traditions of old; she herself was making it obvious that she had a share in the empire her ancestors had won (*Ann.* 12.37.1-6).

Again there is evidence of the theme of freedom versus slavery, which colours both of Tacitus' portraits of Caratacus and Boudicca, and also the literary technique of the 'cross-referencing' of historical personages for the purposes of characterisation; in this instance the picture of Agrippina on an elevated platform nearby, observing the rebel in chains, recalls Cartimandua, the woman responsible for the initial placement of the very chains that led Caratacus to Rome.

Agrippina the Younger, the fourth wife of her uncle Claudius following the execution of Messalina (for the intrigues she and Silius concocted), is the most reviled of all Roman women in the *Annals*. Her usurpation of male authority in the passage concerning Caratacus augments the humiliation inherent in the situation and reduces the power of Claudius, who is consequently feminised. Like Messalina, Agrippina too is a sham Boudicca; the image of her presiding before the Roman standards (*Ann.* 12.37.6) is, as Tacitus points out, *insolitum* (strange) and, as Anthony A. Barrett observes, an example of 'the familiar bugbear of a woman commanding troops' (124).[12] Yet, while Boudicca drives her chariot on the battlefield, assuming masculine authority in a literal sense, Agrippina commands a tame army and a tamed rebel within the bounds of the city. Her actions, nonetheless, are considered by Barrett to possess historical and familial significance for Agrippina herself:

> It would have seemed entirely appropriate to her that the daughter of Germanicus and granddaughter of Drusus, great conquerors in the north-west, should join in presiding over the formal and final (as it would have seemed) surrender of the British (124).

In this sense she functions as a signifier of Roman imperialism and harsh colonialism couched in the patronising garb of clemency.

As symbolic of the process of British servitude as Cartimandua, and as morally corrupt as Messalina, Agrippina is a textual marker of extreme political and ethical degeneracy in the *Annals*. And, as the epitome of everything that is base, she is another imperial woman who symbolises the degeneracy that Rome transports to the provinces – degeneracy against which Boudicca rails:

> ... decency [*decus*], a sense of shame [*pudor*], her body [*corpus*] – everything she [Agrippina] valued less than royal power [*regnum*] (*Ann.* 12.65.4).

Like Cartimandua, Agrippina is marked by her royalty [*regnum*], which Tacitus implicitly associates with inevitable dissolution. As the mother of Nero, she is the direct begetter of further subjugation of the Britons, including Boudicca. Indeed, it is highly significant that Prasutagus bequeaths part of his possessions to her son in the hope that this act of loyalty to Rome would instil in the imperial court a sense of moral duty; but Nero, as the scion of Agrippina, proves to hold no such loyalty.

As with Cartimandua and Messalina, Agrippina destroys the familial unit (for an outrageous additional example, see *Ann.* 14.2 on allegations of her incest with Nero) and thereby significantly disturbs civic leadership and stability, forming another contrast to Boudicca who, following the death of Prasutagus, consolidates the remnants of her family, along with her tribe, and fights for their freedom.

Boudicca and rebel men

While Cartimandua is a leader, a queen, she is not masculine in any way; indeed when she attempts to exercise power (*imperium*), albeit in the form of typically feminine wiles, she instigates the ire of her people, or at least a faction within the vast territory of the Brigantes, who react against her femininity first, her politics second. Even the accounts of the Roman incursions into the disorderly court of Carti- mandua are tinged with the *topos* of 'rescue' in the best tradition of hegemonic masculinity. And while the Romans had clear-cut political reasons for fulfilling Cartimandua's petitions, which makes them far from the saviours of a damsel in distress, Tacitus' portrayal neverthe- less depicts a leader who, because she is a woman, is not fit to rule; accordingly, she really *is* that damsel as far as he is concerned.

In fact, in significant ways, it is Venutius to whom Boudicca may be compared – not his wife – for insofar as they are literary figures in Tacitus' drama, they function as mirror images of each other. For example, both are separated from their spouses (he is divorced and she is a widower) and at the very point of each separation, they take it upon themselves to instigate uprisings against Rome. In addition to an innate ferocity and hatred of Rome, both Venutius and Boudicca are also provoked by personal incentives: Venutius harbours griev- ances against his pro-Roman wife and Boudicca desires revenge for her and her daughters' treatment at the hands of the invaders. The glaring difference is that he is eventually granted rule, while she dies prematurely; had she been taken alive she would have been paraded through the streets of Rome as a female Caratacus. It would also be feasible to suggest that, unlike Caratacus, her life would not have been spared at the end of such a public humiliation, as the emperor was, by then, Nero, not Claudius.

Comparisons can also be drawn between Boudicca and Caratacus in Tacitus' accounts. Caratacus, for all the anguish he caused Rome over the eight years he waged guerrilla warfare is, nevertheless, admired by Tacitus – even if it is somewhat grudging. The battle at Abertanat, which heralded the end of Caratacus' freedom, is de- scribed by Tacitus in *Annals* 12.33-5, and prior to his description of this definitive encounter, Tacitus summarises the words of Caratacus

71

to his troops, which foreshadow the oration of Boudicca leading to the final battle between her forces and those of Paulinus:

> As for Caratacus, he flew here and there, testifying that that day, that battle, would be the beginning of the road to the recovery of freedom [*libertas*] or eternal servitude [*servitus*]; and he called on the names of their ancestors, men who had beaten the dictator Caesar, by whose virtue there was a reprieve from domination and tributes, and who had endeavoured to keep pure the bodies [*corpora*] of their wives and children. Speaking thus, the crowd erupted with every clansman binding himself by obligation to his gods [*religio*] not to capitulate to weapons or wounds (*Ann*. 12.34.2-4).

The image of Caratacus running here and there through the ramparts is recalled in the picture of Boudicca, atop her chariot, approaching each assembled tribe, delivering her battle oration. Caratacus speaks of *libertas* stolen by the Romans and utilises the image of the Britons' fight to keep their collective bodies (*corpora*) pure (*intemerata*). Boudicca stresses that 'The lusts of the Romans had progressed so far that neither bodies, nor age itself, or virginity remained unpolluted (*impolluta*)' (*Ann*. 14.35.2). When compared, the two commanders' expressed anxiety about the corrupted bodies of their fellow Britons reveals a deterioration over time: Caratacus speaks of the desire to keep the collective body pure, whereas Boudicca, nine years later, speaks of the corruption of British purity in endemic terms.

Boudicca and her daughters function as the ultimate example of the powerful theme of the bodies of the Britons corrupted. The Roman invaders are the male equivalents of Messalina. Tacitus' Messalina is the embodiment of corporeal pollution, a living example of tainted sex and death – images symbolised in Tacitus' vignette of her amid the refuse in the cart that takes her along the road to Ostia. She destroys marriages – both her own and others – and she instigates death, actions practised by the imperial forces in the conquest of Britannia. In contrast, both Caratacus and Boudicca symbolise bodily purity and life, the preservation of both being the objectives of their military enterprises. This does not account for the rebel actions of either Caratacus or Boudicca, and Tacitus admits to the latter (*Ann.* 14.33) – yet his condemnation, within the acknowledged *supplicium*, is mild by comparison to that of Dio in his description of the conquests of Camulodunum and Londinium (*Ep.* 62.7). On the other hand, unlike Tacitus, Dio fails to mention Roman military actions in response to British atrocities. While Dio paints the barbarians as barbarians, Tacitus admits that at the final battle between the forces of Boudicca and Paulinus, the Roman 'soldiers showed no remorse in the slaughter of the women, and even the baggage animals were speared and their bodies added to the pile of corpses' (*Ann.* 14.37.4). From the perspective of Tacitus' careful weighing of atrocities on both sides – presented as essentially the natural consequences of warfare – Keegan rightly comments:

> In this context, Tacitus' gendered rhetoric deploys Boudicca as a symbolic representation of how even the stereotypical 'noble savage' (and female in the bargain) can become (or perhaps revert to being) uncivilised when exposed to the least worthy in Roman society (125).

Nevertheless, there is one significant distinction between Boudicca and Caratacus in Tacitus' narratives: the acknowledgement of Caratacus' outstanding mastery of military matters and his silence on Boudicca's abilities in this arena. This is the most explicit instance of Tacitus' gender prejudice in this intratextual reading of the 'British' books of the *Annals*. And while Books 7-10 and parts of Books 6 and 11 are no longer extant, and thus allow no information on Tacitus' treatment of Caratacus, Tacitus declares in Book 12 that 'Caratacus towered above the other British commanders' (*Ann.* 12.33.1). This sits well with the previously cited acknowledgement at *Annals* 12.40.2: '… since the capture of Caratacus, Venutius from the tribe of the Brigantes was [the one] outstanding in knowledge of military matters'. Boudicca never features in any such comparative hierarchy and, despite her portrayal by Tacitus as a figure worthy of empathetic consideration, she cannot be compared to either Caratacus or Venutius when it comes to the science of warfare; bellicose Briton she may be, but she is still a woman.

3

Dio Cassius' Account

Dio Cassius (*c.* AD 165-235) of Nicaea in Bithynia (Asia Minor), a consul at Rome and also a governor of Africa and Dalmatia, wrote a history of Rome in eighty books, of which twenty-six (Books 36-60) are extant. This history, composed in Greek, covers a period from the founding of the city in 753 BC to the year AD 229, with the surviving books treating the years 68 BC to AD 54. Dio's account of the rebellion of Boudicca was epitomised by the Constantinople monk and scholar Joannes Xiphilinus in the eleventh century; indeed, Xiphilinus' version of Dio's Books 36-80 contains useful records of Romano-British relations, beginning with the invasions of Julius Caesar in 55 BC (*Ep.* 39.50-4) and including the only surviving record of Claudius' campaign in AD 43 (*Ep.* 60.19-22).

Like Tacitus, Dio is regarded as a senatorial historian, meaning they both occupied senatorial positions within the imperial system and were, at times, thereby privy to detailed insights and information. As such, they produced work that, in the words of Ronald Mellor: 'was an extension of political life and was aimed at those who held political power in Rome' (2).[1] Dio's political career included work in the provinces, which would 'allow us to conclude that Dio belonged to the inner circle of Severan confidents' (Hose, 462). The change in the reign of Septimius Severus (AD 145-211), marked as it was by the decline in the emperor's relations with the Senate, was likely one of the major motivations behind Dio's decision to focus on the pleasures of compiling history as an adjunct to aggressively pursuing advances in a public career.

Dio is often perceived unfavourably in comparison to others from antiquity, and scholars have sometimes been critical of his style, which is regarded as plodding and dull (according to Eduard Schwartz, to name but one), confused in its conflation of significant and trivial events (according to Fergus Millar)[2] and without structural nuance or complexity. While he may not demonstrate artistic ingenuity or sophistication of design, particularly when compared to the authorial mastery of Tacitus, his material is not always, *pace* Schwartz, completely dry. His portrait of Boudicca, for example, while imbued with the hallmarks of bigotry and imperial sentiment, is nevertheless vivid and certainly memorable – it being a consistent topic in the contemporary accounts of her, be they academic or creative.

In his analysis of the sources for Dio's account of the uprising of the Britons, Townend notes the limited use of the same material that constituted Tacitus' version of corresponding events 'apart from the list of omens ... and the name of the extortionate procurator, Decianus, introduced in rather different connections' (268). Townend argues that the two accounts, by Dio and by Tacitus, are based on two separate main sources, positing that Dio's source is preoccupied with rhetoric and exaggeration, whereas Tacitus' source had a better knowledge of the tactics of Paulinus as well as the resources available to the commander. Somewhat damning of Dio is Townend's summation that 'Tacitus had Dio's main source at his disposal, but found it too uncertain to provide more than a few details' (496). As to this main source, scholars argue against his overuse of Tacitus, and suggest instead the possibility of the afore-mentioned Cluvius Rufus, also a senatorial historian, who was an active politician and scholar during the first century AD, being consul *suffectus* during the reign of Claudius (AD 45), and governor of Spain under Galba (AD 69). However, it seems that Rufus is primarily named as the main source for Dio on the basis that scholars regard them both as problematic historians: they share a tendency to over-exaggerate, they rely on rhetorical flourishes (including generalisations) and they possess a limited grasp of military history. But as Rufus' work is no longer extant and scholars are forced to rely on references to him in the work of others – in addition to the fact that they know the period covered by Rufus included the revolt of Boudicca – it is unwise to ascribe too much influence to him on the basis of assumed similarities between him and Dio (just as it is unwise to argue for the absence of his influence on Tacitus for the opposite reason).

Boudicca's rebellion

From the very beginning, Dio's account of the rebellion is charac-terised by a dramatic, hyperbolic and rhetorical style, illustrated by its fast-paced opening, which captures the suddenness of the uprising:[3]

> ... a catastrophe took place in Britain. Two cities were sacked, eighty thousand Romans and their allies died, and the island was lost to Rome. And in fact, all this was born [*sunenekhthe*] from a woman, a fact that caused them the most shame [*aiskhune*] ... (*Ep.* 62.1.1).

The passage also reveals the focus of Dio's interest – Boudicca (spelt Boudouika in the Greek) – who is to dominate his account of the rebellion at the expense of any mention of the ancillary British leaders. The other major figure in the account is Paulinus, the gover-nor of Britain and Boudicca's nemesis, as the account goes on to reveal. This focus on Boudicca and Paulinus is indicative of what Christopher Pelling has observed in Dio's writing once he 'reaches the early principate', namely that his interest and techniques become 'more biographical' (117).[4]

The Roman defeat is presented as being shameful: Dio's use of the Greek word *aiskhune* (shame, disgrace, dishonour) evokes a sense of moral ineptitude as well as a lack of manly valour. The primary source of this shame is the sex of the victor: a woman was the cause of the military defeat and thus of the Roman and allied disgrace. Dio accentuates the defeat at the hands of a female via the use of *sunenekhthe* from the verb *sumphero*, literally meaning to 'be born' as well as to 'come together' and to 'meet in battle': Boudicca – as yet unnamed – brings forth, or gives birth to destruction and death to the men who face her. Dio continues:

> … indeed, at some point a divine sign gave them an early warning concerning the catastrophe. For at night from the senate-house, barbaric speech along with laughter sounded; and from the theatre clamour with lamentation though no human uttered a sound nor a groan; houses were seen under water in the river Thames, and the ocean between the island and Gaul grew blood-red at the rise of the tide (*Ep.* 62.1.2).

Dio emphasises the role of a series of divine signs of the impending rebellion, a common feature of his writing that, according to Millar, exemplifies his liking for 'tragic history' (43) – stories of supernatural and natural disasters to add emotional depth to the account in question. The reference to the divine signs implies that the gods are on the side of the Romans (mentioned by Paulinus in his oration at *Ep.* 62.11.3), indicative of not only Greek (and Latin) historiographical tradition but ancient literature overall, beginning with Homer's *Iliad*, in which the poet sings of omens such as Calchas' interpretation of the portent of the sparrows and petrified snake at Aulis, interpreted by the prophet as a sign from Zeus that Troy is destined to fall in the tenth year of the war (*Il.* 2.323-32). In a similar vein, and one that matches closely the passage from Dio, Josephus describes comparable sounds before Cassius assassinates Caligula in AD 41 (*Antiq-uities* 19). This prophetic tradition, a central tenet of Greek and Roman belief, pervades the writings of the ancients and often acts as a retrospective interpretation of military and political outcomes as well as revealing specific biases on the part of the authors themselves (the gods will send signs to denote their disapproval at a favourite's impending crisis). The houses seen underwater – kept deceptively vague by Dio, but nevertheless aligning with Tacitus' mention of colonial ruins in the Thames estuary (*Ann.* 14.32.2) – evoke an environment in turmoil reminiscent of more overtly poetic passages from writers such as Ovid who vividly describes fish 'swimming' in trees as a result of the flood initiated by Jove as punishment for unethical human behaviour (*Metamorphoses* 1.296; see also Horace's *Odes* 1.2.9-10). The Ovidian passage is a particularly appropriate comparison as it denotes a world turned upside-down, a reversal of the natural order, as does the account of the impending British uprising against an imperial force, the maintainers of the natural order of things. Of course, in relation to the tumbling statue in Tacitus' account of omens (discussed earlier), such stories should also be considered in their (possible) cultural contexts.

According to Black, Dio's list of portentous events, including the submerged dwellings, 'is dependent on the statement that two cities were destroyed and 80,000 of the Romans and their allies were killed by the rebels and the island was lost to Rome' (416). Black refers to the opening passage (translated above) by Dio (*Ep.* 62.1) that sets the scene, retrospectively, for the havoc that Boudicca wreaked against the Romans. The barbaric sounds recorded by Dio, significantly described as emerging from the senate-house, accentuate the foreign, uncivilised threat posed by the Britons; that these strange sounds are heard coming from within a building symbolically antithetical to barbarian occupation makes the image yet another example of a world turned upside-down. Similarly, the clamour and lamentations from the theatre predict the decimation of Roman forces, lives lost at the hands of Boudicca and her forces.

Dio then immediately proceeds to a brief account of the causes of the uprising. He first mentions a sum of money (*khrema*) that had been made available to the foremost Britons by Claudius (to secure peaceful relations with the Romans) that was being claimed as a loan requiring repayment by the procurator of the island, Decianus (*Ep.* 62.2.1). As Bulst writes: 'The situation suggests that these gifts were called back, because the nobles were now Roman subjects and their loyalty seemed secured' (497). In a similar vein, the second cause is the loan instigated by Seneca the Younger – 40,000,000 sesterces – that was being demanded in full with alleged 'severe measures' meted out to any recalcitrant islanders (*Ep.* 62.2.1). Interestingly, Tacitus, who was aware of the situation with Seneca, as revealed in *Annals* 13.42, makes no mention of it as a mitigating factor in the revolt of the Britons. But these tawdry monetary matters, not impressive reasons for the impending war against Boudicca and her people, are never mentioned again as Dio focuses his attention – and ours – on the 'real' firebrand:

> But the very person who was primarily provoking and persuading them to fight against the Romans, the same person deemed worthy of leadership and who was directing the whole war was Boudicca, a British woman of royal blood, possessing greater intellect than other women (*Ep.* 62.2.2).

Dio highlights the principal role of Boudicca and diminishes the monetary situation as a mitigating factor with the use of the adversative particle *de* (but), the second word in the original Greek sentence. The remainder of the sentence provides a seemingly reasonable or balanced picture of her, particularly in comparison with what is to come: he acknowledges, for example, that she is deemed worthy of leadership, utilising a word commonly associated with men – *prostateia* – to denote the assumption of a public duty or office of great significance. Additionally, her royal origins are attested as is her intellect, the latter denoted by the word *phronema*, meaning both intellect and spirit: as the contrast is being made between her and her fellow women, the translation favours 'intellect' over 'spirit,' but this secondary meaning is also worthy of note, attesting as it does to the force of her nature, her courage and energy. Nevertheless, to balance the good with the bad (with the scales weighted in favour of the latter), Dio makes it clear that Boudicca is the instigator of the unrest and resultant uprising of the Britons against the Romans; she is the *causa belli*. The swiftness and the efficiency with which she assembles her forces, testimony to the use of both *prostateia* and *phronema* in relation to her, are evoked in the sentence that immediately follows:

> This woman lead her army estimated to number 120,000 and ascended upon a raised platform, the foundation of which was constructed in the Roman style (*Ep.* 62.2.3).

Boudicca ascends a speaker's platform (a tribunal), a decidedly male space in antiquity, and the image created by Dio in this briefest of sentences is one of feminine usurpation of masculine authority (as Agrippina did at the trial of Caratacus [*Ann.*12.37.6]): an image of a powerful woman standing *above* and *before* an army of considerable size. As Braund observes in relation to Boudicca (and other female leaders of antiquity): 'An all-powerful man was threatening enough, but an all-powerful woman was awe-inspiring' (118). Braund's analysis is explicitly in relation to Dio's account, and the wondrous terror evoked by Dio's words is derived from the image of her atop the tribunal, preparing to address her forces:

> Her body was exceedingly large [*megiste*], and most ferocious [*blosurotate*] her appearance, and most terrifying [*drimutate*] her gaze, possessing a rough voice, with voluminous yellowish hair down to her

hips, she wore a huge golden twined-collar, a multi-coloured tunic with a thick mantle fastened over the same with a brooch. Thus, in truth, she presented herself, as always. But at this time she had also taken a spear so that she could use it too, to strike universal awe …
(*Ep.* 62.2.3-4).

Dio's account of Boudicca, the only physical description we have, is reminiscent of a Greek or Roman statue of a goddess: the body is larger than life (the Greek word *megiste*, translated here as 'exceedingly large', is frequently used of statues and also of the gods), the overall physicality ferocious (*blosuros* also denotes an appearance that is hairy or shaggy as well as virile or burly) and the gaze 'terrifying' (indeed, Thomas Thornycroft's famous statue of her on the Thames Embankment does honour to Dio's evocation of her presence). Images of Athena (Minerva) or Artemis (Diana) come to mind as one recalls, for example, the devastatingly powerful sculpture of Athena by Pheidias with its eyes made of precious stones, or stories of supernatural statues such as the one of Artemis *Soteria* (Saviour) at Pellene in the Peloponnese that possessed eyes with the power to harm anyone foolish enough to look directly into them; indeed, so powerful was her gaze that when a priestess carrying the statue faced it in the direction of an Aetolian army, the men lost their wits and fled (Plutarch, *Life of Aratus* 32). Numerous accounts in a similar vein are to be found in ancient writing, including references to the power of the Gorgon's eyes in both myth and statuary.[5]

In addition to the power of her gaze, Boudicca is described as possessing a harsh voice, which is possibly a reference to the unpleasant sound of the barbarian tongue to the Greek or Roman ear, or, as Fraser notes:

… again and again the question of the voice will arise. Condemnation of a female leader very often throws in the fact that her voice is harsh and strident. … At the same time approval for a given Warrior Queen frequently takes the form of endowing her with a persistently dulcet tone, in spite of circumstances when any voice, male or female, might be pardoned for being raised (59-60).

Dio's allusion to her alterity is developed further by the reference to her exotic clothing and unruly hair, the latter being a particular sign of a lack of refinement and decorum as defined by the Romans. While the 'large golden ornament' may well be a reference to the torc, a well known adornment of both male and female Celts, Catherine Johns has suggested that the item was no longer common by the first century BC. Subscribing to this theory would lead one to suggest that Dio was adopting a standard literary stereotype of the Britons, that of the torc-wearing exotic, which lasted long after they abandoned the tradition. Nevertheless, there is no definitive answer as to whether or not Boudicca did or did not wear a torc,[6] and perhaps most importantly in terms of Greek historiography, the iconography of the torc definitely accentuates Dio's picture of Boudicca as a fierce and *masculine* warrior, as Johns explains:

> … a gold collar was appropriate for a Celtic leader and warlord … Both literary and artistic references from the Classical world concur in attributing some special power-symbolism to torcs. Torcs formed part of the spoil if a Celtic army was defeated, and we know of a Roman, T. Manlius Torquatus, who earned his name by taking a torc from a fallen Gaulish warrior. Torcs became a recognized form of military decoration in the Roman army (27).

Presenting herself thus, Boudicca addresses the assembled Britons. Her speech is lengthy and detailed and, according to Overbeck, contains 'a long list of conventional complaints and sentiments about slavery and liberty, but nothing that relates to any specific incident involving herself or others' (140). Overbeck's reaction may have resulted in part from the *context* of her speech; the fact that it follows an exotic portrait of a warrior woman may have the effect, for some, of disappointment. Admittedly her words may be read as predictable, following a standard pattern according to the tradition of *parakleseis* (harangues by a general to an army). But in content and style they offer testimony to the intellect Dio ascribes to Boudicca. Additionally, there are several nuanced details that reveal much more than one may glean from a surface reading.

The speech covers several key themes. Boudicca opens (*Ep.* 62.3.1) with the theme of freedom (*eleutheria*) versus slavery (*douleia*) and explicitly intertwines the Roman occupation and the wealth they have introduced into Britain with this theme, thus exemplifying the complexity of imperialism and the outward advantages it brings to the conquered. To her way of thinking, the Romans have deceived some of the Britons with 'tempting promises' (*Ep.* 62.3.1); while vague, her expression indicates that the invading force has promised some kind of financial benefit. Boudicca does not reprimand her audience, or those members of it who may have succumbed to the seductive Romans, but instead tells them that as they have now experienced both *eleutheria* and *douleia*, they are aware of the distinctions between an imported despotism (*despoteia*) and honouring their ancestral way of life. Her combination of the themes of slavery and wealth, and their opposites, freedom and poverty is encapsulated in this excerpt:

'... you have come to know how much superior poverty (*penia*) without a master (*adespotos*) is to being a slave (*doulos*) with wealth (*ploutos*)' (*Ep.* 62.3.1).

Adler, in his analysis of the speech, suggests that Dio's characterisation of Boudicca and the people she represents is in line with the concepts of the 'hard primitive' and 'noble savage' as defined by Arthur O. Lovejoy and George Boas in their 1935 study, *Primitivism and Related Ideas in Antiquity*:

> According to Lovejoy and Boas, 'hard primitivism' is an attitude that uncritically lauds the uncivilized as living in austere conditions, and thus unblemished by the decadent trappings of civilization (Adler, 190 n. 48).

Their scholarly ideas concerning the 'hard primitive' and 'noble savage' are applicable to Boudicca's idealisation of the Britons as an immaterialist community, unaccustomed to the temptations of wealth. The geographical isolation of the Britons, another *topos* of Boudicca's speech, augments the theoretical constructs of Lovejoy and Boas concerning the importance of living on the edges of the known world as a means by which the 'noble savage' escapes the degenerative forces of civilisation. To this end, she envisages the Britons 'as tough, used to enduring hardship and living off the land, whereas the Romans were soft, too accustomed to easy living' (Aldhouse-Green, 138).

Yet in reading Boudicca's words through the eyes of her creator, Dio – the *real* architect of the 'noble savage' motif in this context – the inherent racism and underlying fear of the barbaric 'Other' is revealed. By capturing Boudicca's words in a blaze of rhetoric that eulogises the Britons for their decidedly un-Roman qualities, Dio implicitly underlines their exotic nature (which can be read as their lack of civilisation). His speech, in the mouth of Boudicca, is as strange as her clothing, her overall appearance and her transgendered aura (she is indeed a woman, but she speaks and acts as a man). As with many of the ancient sources discussed by Lovejoy and Boas, the 'noble savage' is defined by contrast with the civilised elite, as the female in antiquity is defined through comparison with the male.

Thus there is a delicious tension in Dio's account that situates the implied reader on side with the author as both participate in decoding the speaker's words.

Boudicca's preoccupation with wealth and possessions continues for a significant part of the speech as she turns to the topic of the loss of property, taxation and tribute:

> 'Have we not been deprived entirely of most of our greatest possessions and do we not pay taxes on the rest? In addition to pasturing and farming all that remains, do we not pay yearly tribute for our own bodies?' (*Ep.* 62.3.2-3).

She equates the yearly payments to the Romans as another example of British servitude and argues that it would have been better to die – to be slain – than to continue to endure taxation, which she equates with financial servitude. The connection Boudicca makes between taxation and slavery, while clearly an example of Dio's flamboyant rhetoric, is not, however, antithetical to the reality of the situation, as Aldhouse-Green observes:

> The taxes were imposed in order to maintain the army, the new Roman towns, like Verulamium and London, and such 'amenities' as the great temple of Claudius at Colchester, built and financed by Britons with loans from Romans like Seneca, the irony being that the British taxes were buying the symbols and realities of foreign domination (137).

The theme of death, introduced in relation to Boudicca's argument that the Britons may well be better off dead than in servitude to the Romans, is elaborated in what may be interpreted as a philosophical style that meditates on the subject of freedom with broader, humanitarian insight:

'By how much would it have been better to have been slaughtered and to have perished than to carry about taxes on our heads? And yet why did I say this? For, with the Romans, not even death has brought release from further payment, but you know how much we hand over for our dead; for among other people, even those living in slavery, death sets them free, but it is the Roman way for the dead to live on for income. Why is it that, though none of us has money (for how or where would we?) we are sold and stripped just as murder victims? And why should they be more moderate in future, when they have treated us this way from the beginning, and when all men treat even newly captured wild beasts well?' (*Ep.* 62.3.3-5).

When read as an example of a more contemplative direction in Boudicca's thoughts, this part of her speech illustrates what Adler detects as Dio's nuanced presentation of his heroine; while far from sympathetic to her plight, his Boudicca is, nevertheless, 'not merely a monster, a barbarian' (191). Thus Adler would argue for a characterisation of gradations that artfully creates a leader worthy of her opponents, which would be more a reflection of Dio's pro-Roman stance than his anti-Boudiccan disposition.

Boudicca's thoughts on the freedom of death also present the reader with a pragmatic side to the leader, admittedly subtly presented, but there nevertheless. While Dio does not have Boudicca mention the will of Prasutagus in this speech, she may well be alluding to the situation that she found herself in following the death of her husband. There is no mention of Prasutagus' will in the actual works of Dio or in the *Epitome*, yet from Tacitus' *Annals* we are informed that his beneficiaries were his daughters and Nero, with the intention that 'this token of submission would put his kingdom and his house out of the reach of harm' (*Ann.* 14.31.1). To a woman who had witnessed the Roman corruption of the good faith her husband had shown both in life and through his will, Boudicca's words concerning the dead remaining 'alive' for the gain of their imperial masters may well be interpreted as a powerful allusion to Prasutagus, his will and the subsequent treatment of both herself and her daughters; women 'sold and stripped just as murder victims' (*Ep.* 62.3.5). This reading suggests that Dio was familiar with the sources, but chose not to include specific details.

The victimisation of the Britons by the Romans, previously exemplified in the speech by numerous references to financial exploitation and the theme of freedom versus slavery, becomes a more central tenet of her rhetoric in the passage that follows:

> 'But, to speak the truth, we are to blame for all these evils (*kaka*), for some of us allowed them to set foot on the island to start with, and did not immediately drive them off, just as we did with the one-and-only Julius Caesar; and we did not deal with them while they were far away as we did with Augustus and Caligula and put to the test a formidable voyage. Therefore, though we inhabit so large an island – or something akin to a continent surrounded by water – and have our own world and are isolated by the ocean from all other people to the extent that we have been believed to inhabit another land and a different sky, and even some of the wisest men have not previously known our name correctly, we have been hated and abused by people having known nothing other than to covet. But although we have not acted justly in the past – oh countrymen and friends and kinsmen (for I use 'kinsmen,' since you inhabit one island and are called by a shared name) – yet at this very moment, let us do so while we remember what freedom (*eleutheria*) is, so that we may bequeath to our children not only its title but also its meaning. For if we utterly forget the good fortune into which we were born, what will these ones do, having been nursed in slavery (*douleia*)?' (*Ep.* 62.4.1-3).

The 'evils' (the powerful Greek word *kaka* is employed) of which Boudicca speaks are cleverly ascribed to the Britons in terms of culpability, thereby augmenting the power of her words within the context of a call-to-arms. In true rhetorical style, she follows her hyperbolic statement with examples from history, naming three Roman leaders: Caesar, Augustus and Caligula. Of the three, obviously Caesar's campaigns in Britain were the most significant, albeit far from substantial (as discussed in Chapter 1). The involvement in the affairs of Britain by Augustus and Caligula hardly compares to the exploits of Caesar, and therefore the naming of them may appear to sit awkwardly when juxtaposed to the latter's imperial inroads, leading Trow to exclaim: 'We would love to know what her grasp of history was' (2003: 139). Boudicca's history is skewed, as Trow implies and goes on to elaborate: 'Augustus made no move against Britain and Caligula's attempt to invade when Boudicca was still a child had ended in a farce' (140). Nevertheless, her inclusion of Augustus and Caligula is not meant to be historically accurate but to illustrate to her audience the Britons' track-record in keeping the enemy at bay.

As we have read between the lines at *Epitome* 62.3, we may do so here, at *Epitome* 62.4, and posit that Boudicca may well be criticising her fellow-Britons because of their failure to act in unison against an invading force, recalling that internal animosities between the tribes meant that the Roman military maxim of divide and conquer was relatively easy to achieve in relation to Britain. Her address to the audience assumes them to be a cohesive force (her repeated use of the plural personal pronoun emphasising the point), which is augmented by the evocation of Britain as an isolated island, a unified, natural entity in and of itself, threatened by immoral invaders. This is skilled rhetoric and if it were anywhere close to the actual words of Boudicca, it is not in keeping with what is known of inter-tribal relations in Britain at the time. Aldhouse-Green succinctly places the rhetoric into historical perspective:

Dio puts into the mouth of Boudica an awareness of a national identity, based on Britain's island status, because it makes a good story and enhances the tale of British rebellion to a grand scale, as though the whole of the province had risen up in arms against their colonial oppressors. The reality is that much of southern Britain, including the islands belonging to Togidubnus, remained loyal to the Romans, and we know that Cartimandua's kingdom also stood firm, despite the anti-Roman sympathies of Venutius (138).

The military insights possessed by Boudicca form the last part of her speech, representing the final theme and portraying her as a well-informed and experienced warrior. Dio maintains the image of her as *the* leader of the Britons with the words: 'thank you for willingly fighting with me and working with each other' (*Ep.* 62.5.1). She goes on to reassure her comrades that they have nothing to fear in fighting the Romans: they are no more numerous than the Britons nor any more courageous; they may fight in full armour but the Britons do not need such protection (an allusion to the well known ancient accounts of the Britons fighting, like all Celtic people, naked). The advantage of fighting on their home territory is also emphasised as is the romantic ideal of the Britons as a people at one with nature and their land, as opposed to the invading force that is depicted as over-civilised to the point of possessing an inability to endure 'hunger, thirst, cold or heat' (*Ep.* 62.5.5). As modern commentators have discussed, the stress on this alleged characteristic of the enemy renders them effeminate in the eyes of the Britons and their leader, and this concept of gender-reversal that colours Dio's portrait of her is inextricably linked with her repetition of the theme of freedom versus slavery, for to be weak and submissive – to be rendered a slave – is for men (and powerful women like herself), to be rendered the weakest of the most stereotypically submissive women.

Following the military harangue, Boudicca performs a ritual in front of the assembled forces:

Having said these things, employing some kind of divination, she let a hare escape from a fold of her dress, and when it ran in an auspicious direction, the whole multitude shouted with delight ... (*Ep.* 62.6.1).

The image of her releasing the hare enabled Dio to further exemplify the exoticness of Boudicca and the very people she commanded (also note Caesar, *BG* 5.12.6, that the hare was not to be eaten, presumably because of its sacred status as an animal used for divination). Sharon Macdonald writes of the incorporation of an act of ritual as part of the characterisation process of the 'Other':

... marginal anomalous figures become hedged around with ritual and taboo which makes us more heedful of the boundaries that our society has laid down. The witch, for example, in being external to normal social categories, becomes a focus for normative social mores (41).

Yet this interpretation requires additional elucidation in keeping with what we know of the people; while Dio is astute in his inclusion of the imagery (indeed to augment her awesome exoticism) and its placement (immediately following the first part of her oration and its function as an interlude before she resumes speaking), we should also acknowledge that the act itself reflects the Britons' belief in augury. While Trow emphasises that the passage should not be taken lightly, for such rites of divination were 'part of their faith' (2003: 144), he gets somewhat coerced by Dio's awe-inspiring portrait, writing: 'the fact that Boudicca carried out what was clearly a ritualistic ceremony implies that she was herself a Druidess with the powers of prophecy to accomplish them' (144). There is, however, no evidence that

Boudicca was a Druid and the interpretation is problematic as there is no definitive evidence for female Druids *per se* (Caesar, for example, specifically refers to male Druids in his account in *De Bello Gallico* 6.14).

Following this hiatus in her speech, Boudicca reinforces her role as leader of the Britons and proceeds to deliver a diatribe against the Romans, focusing on their cultural defects. She raises her hand to the heavens and begins with a salute to Andraste, the indigenous goddess of victory:

'I turn to you, Andraste, and I call to you woman to woman, not leading burden-bearing Egyptians as did Nitocris, nor trafficking Assyrians as did Semiramis (for by now we have learned that from the Romans), nor over the Romans themselves as once did Messalina then Agrippina and now Nero (though he possesses the name "man" he is in fact a woman, hence the markers: singing and lyre-playing and beautification), but [leading] the men of Britain, who do not know how to farm or to practise a trade, but who are experienced in the exact process of warfare, and who hold all things in common – children and women – and thus they possess the same valour [*arete*] as the men. As the queen, then, of such men and of such women, I offer prayers to you and ask for victory and deliverance and freedom against men who are insolent, unjust, voracious, profane, if indeed there is reason to call these men "men" who bathe in warm water, eat artificial delicacies, drink undiluted wine, anoint themselves with unguent, recline on soft couches, among boys, including those past their prime, slaves to an evil lyre-player. Thus, may Lady Nero-Domitia no longer reign over me or you, but let that woman sing to and dominate the Romans (for they think themselves worthy of being slaves to such a woman, having endured submission to her for such a long time), but you alone, o Lady, be our leader always' (*Ep.* 62.6.2-5).

There is very little of an authentic British voice in this last part of the speech; besides the evocation of Andraste, the diatribe against the Romans – particularly Nero – and the references to specific female leaders, is pure Dio. While the Britons may well have had disdain for what they saw as the effeminate Romans – those so-called civilised peoples who took warm baths and engaged in other frivolous physical indulgences – her views on the emperor, in particular, are decidedly literary. This is an especially persuasive reading of the passage in view of Dio's opinions on Nero cited elsewhere (*Ep.* 74.14; 78.13; 80.14), perhaps most notably blaming him for the fire that destroyed Rome (*Ep.* 62.16-18).

Dio exhibits a preoccupation with gender roles and reversals in his portrait of Boudicca in the first part of her speech. In this second and final part of her oration, this anxious fixation comes to the fore in artificial grandeur. His concern at having to narrate a chapter in Roman imperial history that features a barbaric female warrior leads him to grasp for examples of other comparable leaders of the same sex who function, in the opinion of Boudicca, as disastrous case-studies in why women should not rule. As Collingridge observes: 'It was almost as if he had lifted the list of dangerous women from Propertius' Elegy on the enslaving power of love and placed it in the mouth of an Iron Age queen' (257). Indeed, numerous Roman authors, in addition to Propertius, composed works that included lists of the monstrous feminine; Juvenal's *Satire* 6, for example, is a decidedly lengthy poem about the depravity of women that naturally combines outrageous and stereotypical statements with catalogues of evil individuals.

Nitocris, a legendary Queen of Egypt (*c.* 3000 BC), a builder and avenger, was famous for her beauty as well as her devious leadership skills. Semiramis (*c.* 800 BC) took over from her husband Ninus as ruler of the Assyrians; by pretending to be his son, she became renowned not only for her impressive military abilities and successful building programmes, including Babylon (Justin *Philippic Histories* 1.2.1-9), but also for her sexual prowess and its deathly results (selecting the best of her soldiers for gratification, then killing them lest they tell). Her incestuous desires for her son Ninias led to her death at his hands, a somewhat overt comparison with Agrippina and Nero (Justin *Philippic Histories* 1.2.10). These two decidedly Eastern women are juxtaposed to Messalina and Agrippina – Roman power-brokers of the most notorious kind (as discussed in Chapter 2). The placement of their names alongside those of Nitocris and Semiramis gives the *impression* that they were queens, and while Dio's audience would have realised they were not, they would have also conceded that they may as well have been in view of the power they wielded.

The final woman in Boudicca's catalogue is the man-woman, Nero, for, as she claims: 'though he possesses the name "man" he is in fact a woman', as indicated by his 'singing and lyre-playing and beautification' (*Ep.* 62.6.3). Alleged effeminacy, which is inevitably linked with depravity, is a standard motif in ancient biography and historiography of a hostile nature (on Nero, for example, see Suet. *Nero* 29 and 51), and while both Dio and Tacitus are among these unsympathetic sources, the reference to the emperor in the context of the speech above serves a more symbolic function: Nero as imperial leader represents Roman masculinity *in toto*, the slaves being the extension of the master. This is evident in the allusions that follow the diminution of Nero – or Nero-Domitia, as she calls him, the appellation 'Domitia' taking the feminine ending thus functioning as a clever slight at the emperor who was the son of Gnaeus Domitius Ahenobarbus. After rhetorically emasculating the emperor, Boudicca lists the soft lifestyle of Roman men: bathing in warm water, eating impractical foods, imbibing wine that is too strong, smearing their bodies with perfume, lying on cushioned beds and frolicking with boys and young men.[7] Her conclusion is that these so-called men are slaves – not to a leader so-much as an 'evil [*kakos*] lyre-player' (*Ep.* 62.6.4). As Alain M. Gowing perceptively writes in his analysis of Dio's gender-wars in the speech of Boudicca:

… whereas Tacitus apparently wishes to stress that the Romans were indeed disgracefully defeated by a woman named Boudicca, Dio subtly suggests that the woman to whom the Romans owed their defeat was not Boudicca, but Nero (2581).

The Britons, in contrast, are the free peoples under the leadership of Boudicca and, senior to her, Andraste (called Andate at *Ep.* 62.7.3).

After this most powerful evocation of the woman and her words, Dio turns immediately to the battlefield and the atrocities meted out to the Roman settlers at the hands of Boudicca and her forces. The transition from speech to action is swift, thus matching Dio's opening account of the uprising:

> Having spoken thus, Boudicca led her army against the Romans who happened to be without a leader since Paulinus, their commander, had made war upon Mona, an island situated near Britain. Through this situation she pillaged and destroyed two Roman cities and, as I have said, performed unspeakable slaughter. Nothing that was not in itself dreadful was meted out to the captured peoples by them. But the most dreadful and most bestial acts performed were as follows: they strung up naked the noblest and most beautiful women, and then cut off their breasts and sowed them to their mouths, so that to those looking at them they seemed to be eating them, and, afterwards, they then impaled the entire length of the body on wooden stakes. And all this while simultaneously offering sacrifices and banqueting and indulging in illicit acts in their various sacred places and even in the grove of Andate [i.e. Andraste]. This was what they called Victory (*Nike*), and they revered her exceedingly (*Ep.* 62.7.1-3).

When examining the overall treatment of Boudicca by Dio, this passage is arguably the most damning. His description of the forces she led against the people of Camulodunum and Londinium and the atrocities perpetrated against them are particularly horrendous in themselves, but even more so when one reads them without the context that Tacitus provided concerning the Roman treatment of Boudicca and her daughters. While not excusing the inhumanity of the Britons, Tacitus' description of the whipping of Boudicca and the rape of her daughters at the very least balances the scales of cruelty and may be seen to furnish some kind of personal revenge on her part. Rankin, however, discusses the atrocities of the Britons, particularly the treatment of the female corpses, not as revenge per se, but in terms of a ritual or religious response to the Roman invasion, indicative of 'an intrinsic cruelty in the cult of the Celtic goddess of war … [Andraste]. The prospective desperation mentioned by Tacitus may have exacerbated the fury with which they sought further aid from their goddess by means of these sacrifices' (1996: 222).[8] This interpretation is reminiscent of the theory of nativism, the reestablishment or perpetuation of indigenous cultural practices that are re-enacted (especially) in times of threats of acculturation. Stephen L. Dyson utilised this theory in an examination of the British revolts, referring to the Britons' 'state of socio-psychological anguish' (261) at the Roman invasion as necessary consideration in analysing their atrocities, which he defines in part – not as pure revenge, as Tacitus regards them – but as 'characteristic of the early stages of nativistic rebellion' (261).

Characteristically, Dio no sooner mentions Paulinus in Mona than he has him back on the scene, fighting Boudicca and delivering a spirited battle oration to his men (*Ep.* 62.9-11). He explains that the Roman commander had intended to delay battle until a more appropriate season but was pressured into combat owing to food shortages and the ever-encroaching presence of Boudicca's forces (*Ep.* 62.8). In the account that follows, combining Paulinus' speeches and descriptions of warfare, Dio presents a mishmash of narrative, situating the forces somewhere in Britain, presumably in one of his two cities, inadvertently creating a series of vignettes as chaotic as the encounters themselves. In an early scene, Boudicca, riding a chariot, is described as leading an army of 230,000 men and assigning other contingents to designated stations (*Ep.* 62.8.2). Paulinus is described as having far less men, thus being unable to match her line and reluctant to engage in battle for fear of being surrounded and slaughtered (*Ep.* 62.8.3). He apparently separated his men into three divisions to attack the Britons from several points, reinforcing these contingents in order to repel the forces of Boudicca for as long as possible. Where these manoeuvres take place is a mystery.

Nevertheless, from the confusion that is Dio's account of the final battle several pieces of information – however skewed in favour of the imperial forces – may be gleaned. The Romans, for example, are described as focused and orderly, in sharp contrast to the disorganisation of the Britons (whom Dio describes as 'barbarians' at *Ep.* 62.12.1). While the image of these wild, disorganised barbarians had become a trope of Latin and Greek historiography by the time of both Dio and Tacitus before him, it is likely that the discipline, cohesion and leadership of the Roman forces in Britain contributed significantly to their final victory, particularly in view of the fact that the amassed forces of the rebels were recently assembled and lacked the expertise that came with seasons of campaigning.

The battle is described as taking 'many forms' (*Ep.* 62.12.3), situated 'in all three divisions' (*Ep.* 62.12.4) and lasting 'a long time' (*Ep.* 62.12.5). Boudicca is not mentioned during the battle narrative, nor is her adversary, Paulinus. Dio ends the entire segment on the war in Britain with the sudden death of Boudicca, rendered as mysterious as the battle itself, its whereabouts and its intricacies:

> … and then, having died from an illness (*nosos*), Boudicca was mourned terribly and they buried her in lavish style, and at that time, exceedingly broken in morale, they dispersed (*Ep.* 62.12.6).

In contrast to Tacitus' Boudicca, who commits suicide, Dio's Boudicca dies from an illness (whether as a result of poison or natural causes he does not say). Her death is utilised symbolically in Dio's narrative to mark the end of the British rebellion; once their leader is deceased, the Britons, despondent and realising the hopelessness of the situation, leave the battlefield, the implication being that they simply returned whence they came.

Paulinus – a character portrait

While Suetonius Paulinus is portrayed as the Roman's 'man of the hour' in *Annals* 14.33 and is, unequivocally, a powerful and authoritative figure therein, it is the portrait of him in Dio's *Epitome* that is the focus of the following analysis. While Tacitus ascribes in powerful indirect speech, a pre-battle oration to Paulinus (*Ann.* 14.36.1-4), it is Dio's fascinating and detailed creation of the so-called actual words of the general, delivered in direct speech, which shows him to be – literally – the man whose words and deeds lay the groundwork for the definitive process that will inevitably secure Britain for the Romans; as Collingridge writes: 'A military man through and through, Paulinus' goal was to extinguish all resistance and secure Britain for the Romans by whatever force was needed' (178). Delivering a series of impassioned speeches to individual divisions prior to the last encounter between the Romans and Boudicca's forces, Paulinus' words – matching Boudicca's lengthy oration in terms of the structure of Book 62 and in regard to the methodology of characterisation – are imbued with Roman values (via a Greek vocabulary) and the philosophical tenets of imperialism. As a result, Paulinus emerges from the pages of the *Epitome* as a military hero and the Roman general *par excellence*, which runs counter to Tacitus' image of him in the *Agricola* where he is described as impressive in certain respects but also arrogant and at times cruel towards the Britons (*Ag.* 16).

As previously noted, by the time of Boudicca's uprising, Paulinus was the governor of Britain (AD 58-61). His previous military career ensured he was a wise choice for the position, although as David Mattingly has noted, the selection was significantly influenced by the premature death of the previous governor, Quintus Veranius, who died at the end of his first year of office, thus causing Paulinus to be 'brought out of retirement' (178). While this statement may imply that Paulinus was too old for the position, Mattingly also acknowledges that 'the governorship of Britain generally marked the apogee of a general's campaigns' (179), which indeed proved to be the case. Paulinus' experience with mountainous terrain, exhibited by his military command in North Africa in AD 42, during which time he crossed the Atlas Mountains (the first Roman to do so), provided him with the necessary skills to deal with the mountains of Wales and the Brigantian Pennines, which, according to Collingridge would have been considered 'small fry in comparison' (178).

Dio introduces Paulinus into the narrative of *Epitome* 62 after describing the carnage of Boudicca's forces. He describes Paulinus learning of the disasters (*Ep.* 62.8.1) and hastening from Mona to the mainland; however, fearing the numbers and the ferocity of the 'barbarians', Paulinus initially planned to delay battle until a more suitable season. Dio goes on to explain that the delaying tactics proved impossible for the commander to sustain, largely owing to the increasing shortages of food and the activity of the enemy who 'pressed unremittingly upon him' (*Ep.* 62.8.1). Thus confronted, Paulinus is left with no alternative but to face the enemy. Dio summarises the military situation thus:

> Boudicca, leading a cohort of around 230,000 men, having herself mounted a chariot, was directing each band. Paulinus was not able to stretch his phalanx side-by-side, for even if they had been drawn up by ones, they would not have reached far enough to reduce the impact

of the numbers; neither, on the other hand, could he enter the fray for fear of being surrounded and cut back. He was resigned, therefore, to divide the army into three, so they could fight from various points at one and the same time, and he made each one strong enough that they could not be easily broken (*Ep.* 62.8.2-3).

In presenting the back-story to the encounter, Dio stresses the numerical imbalance between the two sides. This effectively lays the groundwork for the impressiveness of Paulinus' victory as well as reinforcing the imperial perspective of the narrative, as G. Fincham observes :

> The number of colonial troops committed to an engagement is usually small and precisely recorded, but by contrast, the natives are numberless, or recorded as suspiciously large round numbers. ... The specific circumstances in which such figures are generated matters less than the fact that it is a commonly repeated pattern, and that such figures originally functioned in a context of colonial conflict for consumption by an imperial audience. ... This has the effect of reducing native insurgents from the status of individuals to simply part of an undifferentiated mass, impossible to define, and thus dangerous when unleashed (27).[9]

Dio records Boudicca's numbers as – in Fincham's words – 'suspiciously large' (Tacitus suggests 100,000) – and as such his account would have had strong appeal to 'an imperial audience', if not a modern one. He also relates the imbalance to Paulinus' deft military strategy; he divides the army into three in order to deal with the (alleged) mass of Britons. And while the image of the Roman forces not being able to stretch across the battle site is vivid and dramatic, creating a powerful spectacle of a grossly outnumbered force amid a vast terrain, it also explains the division of the forces into three, thus enabling Dio to provide three orations for Paulinus.

To his first cohort, Paulinus employs a vocabulary that reduces the 'native insurgents' to non-human opponents, 'from the status of individuals to simply part of an undifferentiated mass' (Fincham, 27) and extols the innate masculinity and humanness of the Roman soldiery:

> Ordering and arranging the soldiers thus, he also spoke: 'Come, men [*andres*]! Come, fellow-soldiers [*sustratiotes*]! Come, Roman men [*Rhomaioi andres*]! Show this plague [*olethroi*] how much, even in our misfortune, we surpass them. It would be shameful [*aiskhron*] now for you to destroy ingloriously what recently you achieved by valour [*arete*]. Let me remind you: in the past both ourselves and our forefathers fought against far greater numbers with far less men than at present – and were victorious. Fear neither their numbers or their revolutionary spirit, nor because they burned a few centres, for their boldness rests on reckless haste and is not based on arms or training and, in truth, they did not take them by strength or after a battle but one was betrayed and the other was abandoned. Demand from them now atonement [*dike*] for these things, and allow them to realise the difference between us, whom they have wronged, and themselves' (*Ep.* 62.9.1-2).

In this powerful opening, Paulinus uses a series of imperatives and vocatives to rouse the adrenalin of his forces, identifying them as *real* men (*andres*), as fellow-soldiers (*sustratiotes*) and as Romans. In contrast the Britons are *olethroi* – that which causes destruction; pests; a plague (significantly rendered in the plural thus conveying the collective singular). The literary conceit is potent: as a force that is huge, and that outnumbers the opponent, the depiction of the Britons as a plague augments the image of a nameless, faceless and inhuman organism of death and destruction. As humans, as men, the Romans are in a natural position to possess human virtues such as *arete* (valour). Dio's use of the latter term situates the Romans in an ethically superior position as human beings and, accordingly, as soldiers, indicating that if the powers of atonement (*dike*) are in operation in the cosmos, they should achieve a moral victory. It is in this sense that Dio's use of the term *olethroi*, becomes even more powerful when juxtaposed to his portrait of the Roman spirit: as the latter are imbued with the essence of *arete*, they are morally pure; in contrast, the Britons, as *olethroi* are symbolically portrayed as polluted in spirit – they are the abject opponent, tainted on the inside just as much as their woad-covered exterior points to their outward 'Otherness'. Therefore, to lose to the Britons is to be tainted with *aiskhron*, that which causes shame, that which is heinous and ugly. These values, namely *arete* and *aiskhron*, have a long literary and cultural history in the Greek world, being employed as early as the Homeric age to define heroes as well as their opposites. Dio thereby taps into a tradition laden with emotional and moral meanings, indirectly calling upon older texts and historical eras/events coloured by such value terms.

Dio situates the present in relation to the past by linking the value terms he includes with reference to the deeds of the Romans' forefathers – in the words of Paulinus: 'Let me remind you: in the past both ourselves and our forefathers fought against far greater numbers with far less men than at present – and were victorious.' The reference to the accomplishments of the ancestors presents one of the core values of the Roman system, namely the responsibility of the Roman man to not only meet the achievements of his predecessors but to surpass them. This is inherent in the Greek understanding of the term *arete* also, but more emphatically conveyed in the Latin terms, *virtus* and *mos maiorum*.[10] Through diligently adhering to *arete*, namely by facing the British hordes bravely and defeating them, the Romans will uphold their duty to the ancestors by expanding an empire that had been established and augmented in previous battles. The fact that the Britons have experienced two previous victories makes Roman conquest in this particular encounter all the more imperative in terms of securing the island for the empire. Paulinus eradicates any concept of military acumen or specialised talent in his reference to previous successes on the part of the enemy, explaining that 'one [town] was betrayed and the other was abandoned'. Extant ancient sources do not provide information on the role betrayal played in the sack of any of the three cities named by Tacitus (Camulodunum, Londinium and Verulamium), although he does explain that Londinium and Verulamium both fell because they were abandoned – upon the order of Paulinus, no less (*Ann.* 14.33) – because he was determined to save the country as a whole rather than risk an overall disaster for the sake of protecting individual centres. At *Epitome* 62.7.1, Dio simply explains that towns fell because Paulinus was at Mona, while the possibility that Paulinus may have had a hand in their abandonment is a subject on which he remains utterly silent – except for the one oblique reference here (*Ep.* 62.9.2). But this is understandably so: to include Paulinus' role in the abandonment of Londinium and Verulamium would be to render this particular part of his first oration embarrassingly ironic. What remains ironic, however, is Paulinus' dismissal of the previous victories of the Britons as simply a case of them burning a few cities (*Ep.* 62.9.2). This sits awkwardly alongside the dramatic introduction to the campaigns of Boudicca at *Epitome* 62.1.1, which summarises it in hindsight as 'a catastrophe' with the death of 'eighty thousand Romans and their allies' resulting in the island being 'lost to Rome'. Additionally, it jars when compared to the description of British atrocities at *Epitome* 62.7.2, which Dio prefaces with the statement: 'Through this situation [Paulinus at Mona] she pillaged and destroyed two Roman cities and, as I have said, performed unspeakable slaughter' (*Ep.* 62.7.1).

Paulinus concludes this first speech with a demand for atonement from the Britons, utilising the powerful Greek word *dike*, which usually translates as justice (rather than 'atonement' as above), to characterise this call-to-arms by a code of honour. His second oration relies less on an appeal to values and more on an emphasis on the benefits of victory:

> 'Now is the time, fellow soldiers, for action, now is the time for courage. If you become outstanding men (*andres agathoi*) today, you will recover what you have lost. If you are superior over them, no longer will anyone else overcome us. Through this one battle you will ensure existing possessions and take over what remains; everywhere soldiers elsewhere will emulate you, and the odious will fear you. Just as you hold in your hands all mankind without fear, both the nations your fathers left you and those you yourselves have added – you could be deprived of them all – so choose to be free, to rule, to be wealthy, to be prosperous – as opposed to enduring the opposite of all this, by rejecting it all' (*Ep.* 62.10.1-2).

He does, however, speak of *agathoi*: men of outstanding character, men who embody strong ethics such as courage and determination, and the physical prowess to put them into practice. As a word utilised by the Homeric poets in both the *Iliad* and the *Odyssey*, *agathoi* refers to heroes, to larger-than-life warriors such as Achilles, Agamemnon and Odysseus, whose actions on the battlefield ultimately shape world history. In keeping with the tenor engendered by the use of this word in the passage, Dio maintains the Homeric tenor of Paulinus' second speech by discussing the enemy as close to, if not equal to, the Romans: 'If you are superior over them, no longer will anyone else overcome us' (*Ep.* 62.10.1). The Homeric concept of fighting one's equal – for in no other way will ultimate glory be bestowed – is inherent in Dio's reading of the Roman mindset. This does not necessarily raise the Britons to any significant status, but is more concerned with idealising Roman prowess, as measured against *Romans* (and Greek heroes) of an earlier era.

The principles espoused by Boudicca in her oration, particularly the theme of freedom (*eleutheria*) versus slavery (*douleia*) at *Epitome* 62.3.1, are echoed in the words of Paulinus. In contrast, however, where Boudicca despises wealth and actively blames the Romans for its introduction into Britain (*Ep.* 62.3.1), being highly critical of its corrupting influences, Paulinus overtly aligns success in battle with the acquisition of capital. Indeed, wealth is equated with success and with empire, and it is through this disjunction between the values espoused by the two leaders that Dio subtly underlines the lack of civilisation on the part of the one, and the embodiment of civilisation on the part of the other. Attitudes towards wealth are construed, in this instance, as an assessment of character and national identity.

In the final speech, Paulinus returns with a heavy-handed application of ethics, combining the value-laden oration with references to the gods:

'You have heard what sort of things these accursed men have done to us – in fact you have seen some of them. Choose then to suffer the same way as the others and be expelled from Britain completely, or prove superior by avenging those who have been destroyed and establish a pattern for the rest of humanity, kindly equity towards the obedient and harsh rigidity towards the recalcitrant. On my behalf, I hope most of all, to be victorious; firstly because the gods are our allies (for they usually support those who have been wronged); secondly, because of the manly spirit [*andreia*] of our fathers, for we are Romans and through our excellence [*arete*] have proved superior to all humankind; next because of our experience (for we have battled and overcome these men who now stand against us); finally because of our honour [*axioma*], for those we struggle against are not opponents but our slaves over whom we conquered when they were free and autonomous. But if the result stands outside our hope (for I will not shrink from mentioning this), it would be better to fall fighting bravely [*andreios*] than to be captured and impaled, to see our innards cut out, to be spitted on red-hot poles, to be destroyed by being melted in boiling water, just as if we had been thrown to lawless and profane wild beasts. Therefore, let us vanquish them or die here. Britain will be a beautiful testimony to us, even though all other Romans here should be driven out. Whatever happens, our bodies will forever possess this land' (*Ep.* 62.11.1-5).

In the preceding chapter on Tacitus' treatment of the rebellion, the concept of a 'just and pious war' was discussed, and in this section of Dio we also feel its influence. Paulinus omits the imperatives and vocatives when addressing the men of the third division, and begins bluntly with the statement: 'You have heard what sort of things these accursed men have done to us – in fact you have seen some of them' (*Ep.* 62.11.1). This immediately sets a tone for the theme of just revenge and situates the principle of a 'just and pious war' within a world context, as Paulinus goes on to extend revenge based on a personal or insular level to the enactment of specific revenge as an example for 'the rest of humanity' (*Ep.* 62.11.2).

Dio's presentation of imperialism in this last speech of Paulinus is reminiscent of the tenets of empire as discussed by Thucydides (regarded as a model for Dio) who, in the words of P.A. Brunt: 'traced Athenian imperialism to three motives, fear, profit and honour' (268).[11] Brunt refers, of course, to the two separate passages in the first book in the *History of the Peloponnesian War:*

'So that at first we were forced to advance our dominion to what it is out of the nature of the thing itself, as chiefly for fear [*deos*], next for honour [*time*], and lastly for profit [*opheleia*]' (1.75.3).

'So that, though overcome by three of the greatest things, honour [*time*], fear [*deos*], and profit [*opheleia*], we have both accepted the dominion delivered us and refuse again to surrender it, we have

3. Dio Cassius' Account

therein done nothing to be wondered at nor beside the manner of men' (1.76.2).[12]

The words are spoken by unidentified Athenian envoys at Sparta in 432 BC who deliver what Clifford Orwin defines as the 'Athenian thesis' on the topic of whether or not the Spartans should start a war against the imperial power.[13]

The theme of fear is certainly present in the words of Paulinus; he begins the speech by reminding the men of the past crimes enacted by the Britons and follows this with an ultimatum: 'Choose then to suffer the same way as the others and be expelled from Britain completely, or prove superior …' (Ep. 62.11.2). The threat is intended to strike fear into the assembled Romans and to thereby inspire them to act in order to preserve their honour and to inevitably obtain, in the long run, some profit from the conquests of empire. The imperative value of honour within the philosophical context of imperial justification is conveyed in Paulinus' words concerning 'avenging those who have been destroyed' as well as in his justification that through the ensuing battle they will 'establish a pattern for the rest of humanity, kindly equity towards the obedient and harsh rigidity towards the recalcitrant' (Ep. 62.11.2).

The confidence Paulinus exhibits in this final speech is based on a series of religious and ethical premises. He believes, for example, that the gods are on the side of the Romans, 'for they usually support those who have been wronged' (Ep. 62.11.3). The idea that the Romans have been wronged is in keeping not only with the theme of a 'just and pious war' but more specifically with self-defence; regardless of the fact that the Romans are in the land of the Britons, Paulinus can still voice this illogical interpretation of the situation, largely because the Britons are savage fighters ('… it would be better to fall fighting bravely [andreios] than to be captured and impaled, to see our innards cut out …') [Ep. 62.11.4]). The manliness [andreia] of the Romans' ancestors, and their own *arete* and honour [*axioma*] are innate collective qualities that further Paulinus' confidence and sense of righteousness.

Dio intends the speeches of Paulinus and Boudicca to be read in comparison with one another; this literary objective is marked by Dio's evocation of certain physical actions that follow specific culminating points in their orations: Boudicca ends the first part of her lengthy battle-call by releasing the hare (*Ep.* 62.6.1); the second part by leading her troops (*Ep.* 62.7.1); so too, Paulinus finishes the last part of his tripartite oration by raising the sign for battle (*Ep.* 62.12.1). The instances where Dio presents their transition into battle – the action that follows the words – is a clear case of deliberate narrative symmetry that links the two leaders; but what is more pointed is the issue of difference, for Dio describes Boudicca's use of staged divination – releasing the hare and observing its path – but includes no such corresponding act for Paulinus. In view of the opening of Book 62, redolent as it is with divine signs and oppressive omens, the absence of any religiosity or related concepts in connection with Paulinus' leadership immediately prior to battle is suggestive of a particular motive on the part of Dio. Whereas Dio imbues the portraits of Boudicca and the Britons with an expressed emphasis on alterity and barbarity, which is communicated in part through the evocation of the former releasing the hare and then calling on the menacing goddess, the Romans, especially their leader, are men who do not dabble in strange omens and pre-battle superstition but are emboldened by the strength of ancestral memories and the sure knowledge that their gods are on their side. Of course, scholars are aware of the intricate and mandatory practices of divination and sacrifice that preceded Roman warfare, so the omission in Dio's account here becomes an overt textual omission carefully designed to reinforce the difference between the Romans and their enemies.

4

After the Ancients: Boudicca's Later Lives

Boudicca has become an icon of British national history and is now a symbol not only of British freedom but also of women's power. She has been painted and sculpted; she has 'starred' in films and has been the protagonist of numerous books, both of an academic and fictional nature. With the revival of all things Celtic – a cultural movement in the West for some thirty years – Boudicca has also come to represent the romanticised Celtic woman; in this manifestation she is rendered utterly fictional in most instances, assuming roles akin to the Druidess, the witch, the matriarch and other unhistorical and invented roles.

Late Antiquity to the Victorian age – an overview

Boudicca's current status as a well-known historical and cultural icon was not always so. When the Roman occupation of Britain resumed in the wake of her defeat, she began to fade from written history, although her memory must have lived on in the oral traditions of her people. The last written reference to her from late antiquity comes from Gildas (*c.* 500-570) in *De Excidio et Conquestu Britanniae* (*On the Ruin and Conquest of Britain*):

> When afterwards they returned to Rome, for want of pay, as is said, and had no suspicion of an approaching rebellion, that deceitful lioness [*leaena*] put to death the rulers [governors] who had been left

among them, to unfold more fully and to confirm the enterprises of
the Romans (6.1-2).[1]

However, E.A. Thompson dismisses an allusion to Boudicca via the
term *leaena* (lioness), preferring to interpret it as a reference to Britain,
which he bases on Gildas' use of the word elsewhere to denote a
country (204).[2] Others, Hingley and Unwin, Collingridge and Aldhouse-Green, interpret *leaena* as a reference to Boudicca which, as
Hingley and Unwin thereby suggest, 'may demonstrate that knowledge of her actions survived in Britain after the fall of the Western
Roman Empire' (61).

While scholarly interpretations vary on this point, there is little if
any ambiguity concerning her absence from accounts of early British
history that follow closely on from Gildas. Indeed, testimony to her
disappearance from written history is her absence from Bede's *Historia ecclesiastica gentis Anglorum* (*The Ecclesiastical History of the People of
Britain*, or *HE*), composed around 731; even though Bede mentions
the Claudian invasion (*HE* 1.3) and that two towns were taken and
destroyed in the reign of Nero, there are no details concerning
Boudicca. Similarly, Nennius' *Historia Brittonum* (*History of Britain*),
written in approximately 830, and Geoffrey of Monmouth's *Historia
Regum Britanniae* (*The History of the Kings of Britain*), written in approximately 1136, make no mention of her.

It seems that Boudicca's reintroduction into the annals of history
was through the Italian historian, Polydore Vergil (*c.* 1470-1555), who
wrote of her as 'Voadicea' in his *Historia Anglica* (officially released in
1534), a work commissioned by King Henry VII. And as the Renais-
sance took hold and the works of antiquity began to be revived,
Boudicca began to re-emerge from the shadows of history and
reassume her status as a figure who demanded attention. In Hector
Boece's *Historia Gentis Scotorum* (*Chronicles of Scotland*) published in
1527, she is not the historical figure we know but 'Voada', a woman

from northern Britain, sister of Caratak (Caratacus) and Corbreid, the kings of Scotland (Macdonald, 46). Both Polydore and Boece acknowledge their use of Tacitus, although they make no mention of Dio, and, while it is not entirely unfeasible that they were aware of Xiphilinus' *Epitome*, Boece did not read Greek, and does not utilise specific elements from the narrative. Indeed, according to Samantha Frénée-Hutchins:

> It seems then that Dio's source was first referred to by the Welsh cartographer and antiquarian, Humphrey Llwyd (or Lhuyd, 1527-1568) in his Latin manuscript, *Commentarioli Brittanicae descriptionis fragmentum*, finished in 1568. This was published in Cologne in 1572 and then translated into English by Thomas Twyne and published in London the following year under the title, *The Breuiary of Britayne* (32).

Polydore's Boudicca is fascinating, particularly because of the portrayal of two women – Voadicea, a queen from the north, and Bunduica, a wild and savage warrior capable of the most gruesome crimes in her campaign against the Romans. Jodi Mikalachki suggests that the provision of two women perhaps resulted from the difficulties Polydore found in 'reconciling the ancient queen's savagery with her patriotism, as well as from the manifold versions of her name in classical sources' (119). Boece's Boudicca is perhaps more consciously subversive, especially in its inherent inventiveness. This could well be the result of the remnants of an oral history, described by Lewis Spence as 'that great mass of floating tradition which appears to have grown up in Britain around the circumstances of its early association with Rome' (159) and their access to other unusual versions that were also, no doubt, the products in part of an active oral tradition. Boece, for example, has Voada as wife of one Prince Arniragus of Wales (decreed King of the Britons by Claudius); sister of Caratak (Caratacus); mother of two daughters and one son. There are several domestic troubles in Boece's story, including Arniragus' affair with a Roman woman and his departure from the family unit – although he later returns to Voada, denouncing the Romans at the same time, and thereby setting in motion renewed hostilities between the two peoples. While Boece's narrative is unhistorical, it is indicative of the era in which it was composed and the burgeoning need for the Britons to re-embrace Boudicca. Thus it is a new version of her in keeping with Christian faith, the ethical and social position of British womenfolk, and a national identity and concept of nationhood within a broader European context. The birth of a new Boudicca is evident in Boece's writing; situated safely within a domestic and familial unit, she is a woman before she is a heroine, a wife and mother before she is a lioness.

Inevitably, the well-known story of Tacitus appears in Boece's narrative: Voada, having been thrashed by the Romans, and having been witness to the rape of her daughters, goes to battle. However, she does not lead the men, but is the head of a band of ladies. Always loquacious, she delivers a speech before leading the good women of Scotland to war:

> 'The proud Romans may know what vassalage ladies may do when extreme danger occurs. And though I may no wise devoid me of wifely image, I shall not lack men's hardiness, but armed foremost in the brunt, where most danger appears, with 5,000 British ladies who were all sworn to vindicate their injuries, we shall proceed foremost in battle, not regarding fear of death, or bloody wounds or terrible slaughter of ourselves or enemies; for I can have no commiseration with those who pursued my tender friends with such cruelties, deflowering so many virgins and matrons by effeminate lust, putting so many rich cities and towns to subversion, and innocent people to murder.'[3]

Voada stresses that she fights as a woman on behalf of women; long gone are the shades of masculinity attributed to the Boudicca of Tacitus and Dio. Like Tacitus' Boudicca (*Ann.* 14.37), however, Boece's heroine commits suicide rather than be captured following the defeat of the rebel forces. It is one of her daughters, Vodicia, who continues the fight, although she is eventually captured and executed.

Raphael Holinshed wrote of her in his *Chronicles* (1577), an Elizabethan text that typified the increasing fascination with Boudicca that was partly the result of the reign of another powerful English woman, Elizabeth I. Yet, just as Polydore struggled with the image and iconography of Boudicca – resorting to dissecting her, literarily speaking – so too did the authors of the Elizabethan era. Fascinated with the opportunity of flexing some impressive literary comparisons between the two queens, writers still needed to reconcile the British freedom-fighter and historical queen *par excellence* with the blood-thirsty mutilator in order not to offend the Virgin Queen to whom she was being compared. As Frénée-Hutchins observes: 'It is presumably because of the darker side to Boudica's religious activities that she was not appropriated to the same extent that the Virgin Mary was' (145). Frénée-Hutchins is of course referring to Boudicca's dealings with Andraste as recorded by Dio, an account that even the most gifted literary artist would find challenging to rewrite, and which leads her to conclude that the Andraste association more than likely accounts for 'why Elizabeth was more often compared to the prophetess Deborah than to Boudica' (145).

One of the earliest comparisons between Elizabeth I and Boudicca comes from Stephen Gosson (1555-1624) in a pamphlet entitled the *School of Abuse* (1579). Gosson utilises Dio's version of Boudicca's speech in order to cast aspersions on the contemporary degeneracy of English men, particularly those in power. The comparison between the two women is somewhat opaque but nevertheless present; he praises Elizabeth but criticises the men around her, contrasting them with the burly, hardy and brave men who fought alongside Boudicca. The portrait of Boudicca is positive, which makes it a significant milestone in the literary history of post-antique representations, as Hingley and Unwin write: 'In Gosson's account, Bunduica appears to be a positive figure, even though she evidently did not possess the power of the majesty of the contemporary queen' (119). Elizabeth herself embraced the comparison with political *savoir-faire*, seizing a very public moment – the sailing of the Armada – when she visited the troops at Tilbury in 1588, to deliver a speech worthy of her predecessor.[4]

The comparisons between the two queens ensured that Boudicca eventually re-entered British history as a positive icon of national identity. There were, of course, dissenters such as John Fletcher whose drama, *Bonduca* (1610), did not show her in a favourable light (to say the very least), illustrating the problematic tension of gendered history, which, despite Elizabeth's reign, would take at least another century to dissipate. By the late seventeenth century there was still the overriding imperative to preserve British history as a prevailingly androcentric process. By the eighteenth century, however, the male anxiety that characterises literature such as Fletcher's began to erode, replaced by sentiments such as those expressed in William Cowper's 'Boadicea, an Ode' (1782):

> When the British warrior queen,
> Bleeding from the Roman rods,
> Sought with an indignant mien,
> Counsel of her country's gods.
>
> Sage beneath a spreading oak
> Sat the Druid, hoary chief
> Every burning word he spoke
> Full of rage and full of grief.

'Princess, if our aged eyes
Weep upon thy matchless wrongs,
'Tis because resentment ties
All the terrors of our tongues.

Rome shall perish – write that word
In the blood that she has spilt;
Perish hopeless and abhorred,
Deep in ruin and in guilt.

Rome, for empire far renowned,
Tramples on a thousand states;
Soon her pride shall kiss the ground,–
Hark! The Gaul is at her gates.

Other Romans shall arise,
Heedless of a soldier's name,
Sounds, not arms, shall win the prize,
Harmony the path to fame.

Then the progeny that springs
From the forests of our land,
Armed with thunder, clad with wings,
Shall a wider world command.

Regions Caesar never knew
Thy posterity shall sway,
Where his eagles never flew,
None invincible as they.'

Such the bard's prophetic words,
Pregnant with prophetic fire,
Bending as he swept the chords
Of his sweet but awful lyre.

She, with all a monarch's pride,
Felt them in her bosom glow,
Rushed to battle, fought and died,
Dying, hurled them at the foe.

Ruffians, pitiless as proud,
Heaven awards the vengeance due;
Empire is on us bestowed,
Shame and ruin wait for you!

Cowper's ode, pregnant with its own historicity – bespeaking as it does of the burgeoning empire – makes the powerful and long-lasting association between Boudicca and British imperialism. The opening lines are testimony not only to Cowper's talent as a poet but also to the awe-inspiring and by then well-established reputation of his persona: at line one she is introduced as 'the British warrior queen', which is powerfully contrasted with the imagery of her at line two where we find this woman of royal heritage 'Bleeding from the Roman rods'. Boudicca as a martyr of British freedom is symbolically juxtaposed to the iconic figure of the Druid who is introduced at stanza two, a figure who is described as 'burning' as his queen was described as 'bleeding'. The Druid predicts the fall of Rome via allusion to the Visigoths (stanza five) and the replacement of the Roman empire with new world powers (stanza six). The ultimate imperial power will be the very people the Romans have suppressed so ruthlessly – the Britons – whose 'progeny' shall rise from the very forests that have been destroyed by the invaders (stanza seven). Cowper's Druid, imbued with nationalistic fervour, delivers a pane-gyric to his nation's imperial success, emphasising that its borders now surpass that of the Roman territories (stanza eight). These lengthy words of prediction, delivered to Boudicca after she has been whipped by the Romans, spur her on to fight, leading her people against the forces of oppression. Thus empowered she enters the fray, only to encounter death. The image of Boudicca rushing to battle, fighting and dying – delivered in one brilliantly concise line in stanza ten ('Rushed to battle, fought and died') – accentuates the image of her that was to be so wholeheartedly embraced by the Victorians, namely that of the legendary and larger-than-life warrior queen of *England*. In the true style of dramatic narrative poetry, Cowper saves his queen from ultimate defeat by concluding the poem with an ill-omened message to the Romans: 'Empire is on us bestowed, / Shame and ruin wait for you!' The freedom-fighter, the rebel, has become the imperialist; the oppressed has become the oppressor. In the context of British history, Cowper's poem is a powerful artefact of a 'moment' in time, as Hingley and Unwin comment:

> The poem was published at a time of British territorial expansion and political ambition following a period of lengthy conflict, including the American War of Independence, and Boadicea was adapted to fit this context. The poem helped to project Boadicea into the context of the British Empire by suggesting that her actions had assisted with the development of British imperialism, effectively creating her as an imperial icon (150).

It is not surprising, then, that Thomas Thornycroft's monument to Boudicca – arguably the ultimate example of the symbolic connection between her and British imperialism – was accompanied by two lines of Cowper's poem: 'Regions Caesar never knew/ Thy posterity shall sway.'[5]

In his tribute to the warrior queen, published in 1864 with the title 'Boadicea', Alfred Lord Tennyson allows Boudicca words of her own. After establishing a historically accurate scene, with the Roman troops at Mona and Boudicca in the east of England (stanza one), Tennyson describes her mounted upon a chariot alongside her daughters, delivering her own script:

117

'They that scorn the tribes and call us Britain's barbarous popu-
  laces,
Did they hear me, would they listen, did they pity me supplicating?
Shall I heed them in their anguish? shall I brook to be supplicated?'

In this excerpt, which opens stanza two, Tennyson reveals his grasp
of the ancient sources; he echoes the Greek and Roman accusations
of barbarism, he conveys both Boudicca's anger at the enemy's
negation of her grievances and her righteous indignation at her
humiliation, and rhetorically and ironically questions her own response to their impending doom at her hands. Tennyson's Boadicea
is a woman of vengeance, a woman aligned with the justice espoused
in the Old Testament, who is hell-bent on smiting her enemies
without remorse. The hostility between the two sides is accentuated
in this stanza by the inclusion of animal totems: the sharply taloned
eagle of the Romans, along with their 'wolf and wolfkin' do battle
with the English hare and raven 'Till the face of Bel be brighten'd'.

Composed during Tennyson's time as Poet Laureate, 'Boadicea' is
characterised by the prescriptions of national poetry; it is overtly
patriotic and firmly reflective of the empire under Victoria in terms
of national pride, confidence and identity. While scholars have written on Victoria and Boudicca as two of the most iconic queens of
Britannia, there has been little comparison of Tennyson's specific
Iron Age queen and the monarch of his own time. Tennyson's
Boadicea is bloodthirsty, battle-driven and far removed from the very
'Victorian' Victoria whose rule was couched in a public diplomacy
and grace that habitually veiled the harsh realities of British imperialism. Despite the somewhat unpalatable elements of what is, arguably,
Tennyson's most experimental poem (and certainly one of the least
popular),[6] it does contain some stirring material, in keeping with the
tenor of 'Rule Britannia':

So the silent colony hearing her tumultuous adversaries
Clash the darts and on the buckler beat with rapid unanimous hand,
Thought on all her evil tyrannies, all her pitiless avarice,
Till she felt the heart within her fall and flutter tremulously,
Then her pulses at the clamouring of her enemy fainted away.
Out of evil evil flourishes, out of tyranny tyranny buds.
Ran the land with Roman slaughter, multitudinous agonies.
Perish'd many a maid and matron, many a valorous legionary.
Fell the colony, city, and citadel, London, Verulam, Camulodune.
(sixth and final stanza)

Boudicca's historical depictions in the field of reception have so far revealed the Anglo-British struggle to incorporate her within their progressive reconstruction of history. From the silence of the scholars of late antiquity, to the damning reference by the pro-Roman Gildas, the fanciful stories of Boece and the gendered-based tensions of the Elizabethans, it is not until the modern era – inspired by the poetry of Cowper and Tennyson and the monument of Thornycroft – that her status as the archetypal British heroine would be restored. This shift toward a reverential attitude would set the scene for a further alteration, one that continues through to the present day, and the first to be spearheaded primarily by women.

The women's Boudicca – a feminist icon

From Thornycroft onwards, changes in the representations of Boudicca began to make their presence felt as more personalised images of her emerged. Indicative of the increasingly cultural move in the west for individualised use of national icons, artists made Boudicca in their own image and likeness to express private emotions, opinions, wants and desires. What is characteristic of these later receptions is the marked gender divide between the artists and their creations; indeed it is relatively easy to detect the gender of the maker in most instances before their identity is even revealed.

In terms of the fantasy genre, male artists tend to portray Boudicca as a siren or sex-goddess and/or a passive, ultimately defeated 'heroine', painting and digitally manipulating images of her that are hyper-sexual and thus far-removed from what we know of the historical figure.[7] One exception to this (general) rule is the portrait of Boudicca by Alexia Sinclair in her series entitled 'The Regal Twelve'. Sinclair, an art photographer and digital artist, depicted twelve historical women, including Cleopatra, Agrippina, Catherine the Great and Elizabeth I, in a much-lauded enterprise that has received worldwide exposure, including a showing at the 2009 Paris Biennale. While the techniques behind these portraits are exquisite and they are undoubtedly beautiful to look at, there are numerous ethical – let alone historical – issues worth examining. In the portrait of Boudicca, for example, the figure looks little more than a glossy porn star: exceedingly young, Boudicca appears to have had the advantages bestowed by a dedicated team of make-up and hair stylists (she has clearly had hair extensions), while her pose suggests she is about to embark on a highland fling. In an example of postmodern art gone mad, she not only wears a kilt (and flesh-coloured tights), but is topless yet helmeted. As a tribute to a woman who was abused, saw her daughters raped before her eyes, and led an army to save her land and her peoples from foreign despotism, Sinclair's portrait is problematic in its portrayal of Boudicca as a modern icon of middle-class gallery consumerism: pretty, vacuous and sexualised.

In terms of her use for personally-driven artistic means – by which the artist 'exhibits' his/her own message(s) – Judy Chicago's inclusion of Boudicca in her renowned feminist installation, *The Dinner Party*, is an early example of the appropriation of the British icon for feminist purposes. 'Boadaceia place setting' is one of thirty-nine dinner settings depicting thirty-nine different mythical and historical women (with the names of an additional 999 women inscribed on the porcelain tiles on which the triangular dinner table rests), produced by Chicago and her art collective from 1974 to 1979. As with all the 'seated' guests, Boudicca's setting is mixed-media, consisting of an individual table cloth or runner and a plate (among other items); her fabric is embroidered with stereotypical Celtic patterns, which according to Chicago 'signify both personal strength and the Roman encroachment upon her autonomy and power' (80).[8] Her plate is framed with Stone Age pillars recalling Stonehenge and evoking her mysterious origins (particularly to the modern, Western audience); and a golden helmet, unadorned yet stylised, sits in the middle as testimony to her role as warrior. As with many of Chicago's designs on the dinner-plates, Boudicca's plate is also imbued with allusions to female genitalia, with the rounded columns of her faux-Stonehenge evoking thick labia and the helmet symbolising the internal sexual organs.

As a feminist icon, Boudicca has long been utilised by women for political ends, particularly for a socio-sexual agenda of the like demonstrated by Chicago. In her 1984 work entitled *Another mother tongue: gay words, gay worlds*, for example, Judy Grahn posited – incorrectly, but provocatively – that the word 'bulldyke', a modern term for a butch lesbian, originated from the name 'Boudicca' (136-9). Grahn's claim reveals the feminist appropriation of Boudicca albeit via an unsettling, earnest etymological belief that reflects the sometimes unstable results that emerge when sexual and gender politics override common sense.[9]

Women's appropriations aside for a moment (but rebel appropriation to the fore), Boudicca as an icon of freedom and left-wing political art and ethics is perhaps best represented in recent times by the 'utilisation' of Thornycroft's monument by underground artist, Banksy. In 2005 Banksy placed a bright yellow clamp on the wheel of her chariot, which remained untouched for a mere twelve days.

Boudicca's chariot wheel, clamped by Banksy. © Pest Control Office 2010.

Indicative of Banksy's street installations, the clamp represented his views on public space and the political mentality behind monumental art, as revealed in the following aphorisms by the artist:

> If you want someone to be ignored
> then build a lifesize bronze statue of
> them and stick it in the middle of town.

> It doesn't matter how great you were,
> it'll always take an unfunny drunk
> with climbing skills to make people
> notice you.[10]

Banksy is not the only activist who works 'with' and 'against' Thornycroft's monument. In 2009 a collective of protesters called 'Climate Rush' adorned the statue with a red and white poster reading 'DEEDS NOT WORDS / CLIMATERUSH' and tied a matching red ribbon to Boudicca's neck. The acquisition of the statue and the space around it for means of political insurgency recalled the Suffragettes, an acknowledged source of inspiration in this instance, who also reclaimed and/or reinterpreted Thornycroft's Boudicca. Suffragette Dora Montefiore (1851-1933), for example, recalled in her autobiography:

> One of my best meetings was close to the statue of Boadicea in a prohibited part of London, as no meetings were allowed to be held so close to the Houses of Parliament. It had long been my wish to hold a meeting there, as Boadicea in her chariot always appeared to me to be advancing threateningly on the Houses of Parliament, and she was therefore a symbol of the attitude towards Parliament of us military women. Toward the end of 1906 tramlines were being laid at that part of the embankment, and the traffic was obstructed by piles of wood blocks, and these I saw would make a most capital rostrum from which to speak.[11]

'Boudicca agrees, DEEDS NOT WORDS.' Photo: tim.dalinian.jones@gmail.com, copyleft: CC BY-NC-SA 3.0.

While it has been recorded that Montefiore spoke for well over one hour, we do not know what she said, but in view of her location and her autobiographical musings some 21 years later, she very likely drew connections between Boudicca and the Suffragettes. Hingley and Unwin in their study of Boudicca comment on Montefiore's attachment to the site, suggesting that the 'fact that she gave this speech from a wooden platform, or tribunal, may suggest that she drew directly upon Dio's account of Boudica' (175).

Sylvia Pankhurst (1882-1960), a leader of the Women's Social and Political Union (WSPU) from 1906-1914, recalls a particular march in May 1906, which 'started from the Boadicea statue on Westminster Bridge', reflecting the use of the statue and its locale as a symbolic rallying point for the women's rights movement during the first part of the twentieth century.[12] Pankhurst also mentions media coverage of another protest, namely the report on the rally on 21 June 1908, described by the *Daily Express* thus:

> The Women Suffragists provided London yesterday with one of the most wonderful and astonishing sights that have ever been seen since the days of Boadicea. ... It is probable that so many people never before stood in one square mass anywhere in England.

At this protest, women from the National Union of Women's Suffrage Societies (NUWSS) carried banners of silk and velvet made by the women of the Artists' League, which depicted great women from the past, including Boudicca. And on 17 June 1911, women from the WSPU, along with other Suffrage societies, dressed as famous heroines, once again including Boudicca, and marched *en masse* through the streets.[13] But this employment of dramatic spectacle for political empowerment was perhaps best illustrated in *A Pageant of Great Women*, which opened on 10 November 1909 at the Scale Theatre in London. Conceived and produced by the Actresses' Franchise League, the pageant was written by actress, writer and suffragette, Cicely Hamilton (1872-1952), and directed by Edith Craig (1869-1947), daughter of Dame Ellen Terry (1847-1928), and a well known producer and theatre designer in her own right. The *Pageant*, which went on to tour the country, featured great women from history – Joan of Arc, Elizabeth I, Catherine the Great and Florence Nightingale – with the role of Boudicca (Boadicea) played by Elizabeth Kirby (see Fraser 300-1; Hingley and Unwin 75-6).

On such appropriations and adaptations of Boudicca as a symbol of women's freedom – and oppression – Hilda Kean writes:

> The historical iconography of suffrage specifically included past heroines, such as Grace Darling, Florence Nightingale, Harriet Martineau

and Mary Wollstonecraft as well as the military figures of Boudicca and Joan of Arc, examples of both militant women and those who died for their cause.[14]

Supporters of the cause made comparisons between the female freedom fighters and Boudicca as revealed in this extract from the writings of Australian feminist, novelist and essayist, Miles Franklin (Stella Maria Sarah Miles Franklin, 1879-1954):

> Mrs. Emmeline Pankhurst has been in our midst, petite and daintily dressed, fearless and outspoken, indomitable as a Boadicea, irresistible as a fairy.[15]

It seems ironic to a modern person to read a sentence that uses similes of both Boudicca and a fairy to describe someone, for the two types of femininity evoked seem eons apart. Nevertheless, Franklin's summation of Pankhurst, so deftly evoked in this one sentence, embodies the paradox at the very centre of the public image of the Suffragette woman, as Bartley notes:

> Emmeline Pankhurst, and the other suffragettes, seemed to be a paradox: beautifully dressed and coiffured while at the same time rejecting other feminine values. It is this paradox which appeals: the suffragettes' physical *appearance* was the very essence of femininity whereas their violent physical *actions* challenged and undermined Edwardian notions of that same quality of being female. On the one hand, suffragettes conformed to the romantic ideal of womanhood by paying a great deal of attention to appearance and wearing white flimsy dresses with violet corsages. On the other hand, they challenged the very essence of womanhood by their militant behaviour (109).

The seeming contradiction in terms inscribed on the public body of a woman such as Pankhurst recalls the anxieties inherent in the

A Pageant of Great Women, 1909: left to right: Joan of Arc, Boadicea,
the Rhani of Jhansi and Agnes Dunbar.

historical tradition concerning the representation of Boudicca from
the time of Tacitus onwards. Indeed, like the writers who struggled
with what they regarded as a disjuncture between Boudicca's female
body and the socially-constructed attributions of masculinity, the
opponents of the Suffragettes also muttered about such violation of
nature. Pankhurst wanted to 'feminise politics, not to masculinise
women who wished to be engaged in political activity. Equally, she
was defensive about the accusation that suffragettes were unnatural
and mannish' (Bartley, 109). In this way, her subtle refining of gender

stereotypes was explicitly understood by Franklin whose similes speak so concisely of the complexities inherent in the challenging task of women occupying the public space.

What is fascinating in a comparative study of the Suffragettes and Boudicca is the similarity in the chroniclers' accounts of their physicality. Dio describes Boudicca as large, physically threatening (read masculine or a female-male hybrid) with a coarse voice, while in a parody written by activist Mary Phillips in 1907, she describes the generic or stereotypical Suffragette as:

> ... [a] gaunt, unprepossessing female of uncertain age, with a raucous voice, and a truculent demeanour, who invariably seems to wear elastic-sided boots, and to carry a big 'gampy' umbrella, which she uses as occasion demands either to brandish ferociously by way of emphasising her arguments, or to belabour any unfortunate member of the opposite sex who happens to displease her.[16]

The woman occupying the public space, a decidedly masculine terrain in the early years of the twentieth century, is problematic for the conservative onlooker; hence she must be relegated to a 'safe' or comprehensible form of interpretation. As Boudicca carried her spear to attack the Roman soldiers, Phillips' unfashionable and unladylike Suffragette carried her tattered old umbrella as a weapon to assault any hapless males who crossed her path. Boudicca lived on, not just in the minds of women like Pankhurst, but in the anxieties of her opponents.

S.D. Shallard of the Fabian Society, in an essay entitled 'Women in War', in the periodical *Votes for Women* (7 August 1914), wrote:

> It is hardly necessary to recall the fact that, after infamous treatment by Nero's procurator, Boadicea took the field against the Romans with a force that included five thousand women, nearly all of whom died fighting.[17]

4. After the Ancients: Boudicca's Later Lives

A supporter of the Suffragettes, Shallard, like Franklin (both writing at roughly the same time), calls on the simile of Boudicca in his discussion of women's willingness to participate in war. Written in the month that World War I broke out, Shallard's article anticipates the social and ethical issues confronting women in Britain as a result of the war, probably aware that a faction of the women's movement supported it. Some Suffragettes, for example, were adamant supporters of World War I, believing it was a woman's duty to support her country and the men who were fighting for it.

On a more typically 'feminine' note, and once again in the spirit of Boudicca, Suffragettes could buy brooches depicting her, as recalled by Bessie Watson, arguably the youngest protester in the British movement:

> A few weeks later Christabel Pankhurst came to Edinburgh to address a meeting at the King's Theatre and I was invited to attend. During the evening I was presented with a brooch representing Queen Boadicea in her chariot, as a token of gratitude for my help in the pageant.[18]

Bessie received the brooch as a result of playing the bagpipes for a WSPU historical pageant on 9 October 1909 in Edinburgh; she was nine years old. As an old woman, Bessie gave the brooch to Margaret Thatcher when she became Prime Minister in 1979. This is a somewhat ironic and indeed absurd gesture on the one hand, yet utterly appropriate on the other, for Boudicca means different things to different people. While she can be interpreted as a freedom-fighter and rebel, an underdog and victim who refused to be victimised, she also became the symbol of British imperialism and hence ultra-conservatism. Banksy's wheel clamp is a mockery of the latter concept while simultaneously acknowledging the poignancy of her outsider status to the English, which, as his symbolic gesture suggests, is nowadays forgotten (save for protesters like Climate Rush).

The conservative politics of the conservatives' Boudicca was

129

Caricature by George Gale, *Daily Telegraph*, 11 June 1987,
© Telegraph Media Group Limited 1987.

embraced by, and parodied in, the critical cartoons of Thatcher;
George Gale, for example, drew a caricature of her as the British
heroine, published in the *Daily Telegraph* on 11 June 1987 in response
to her triumph at the polls for a third consecutive term. During the
Falklands War, political opponent Denis Healey described her as
'charging about like some bargain-basement Boadicea'.[19] Healey's
description of the Prime Minister not only overtly comments on
Thatcher's past depictions as Boudicca but may also be a dig at her
'heritage' as the daughter of a grocer. The references to Boudicca are
particularly salient in relation to Thatcher as she came from Northamptonshire, one of the areas at the centre of the Boudiccan
rebellion, it being the country of the Catuvellauni, with Watling Street
passing through the county. The comparison, which was always
meant to depict Thatcher negatively – as some marauding warrior
queen drunk on her own power – sat alongside the other female icon
regularly associated with her: Britannia.

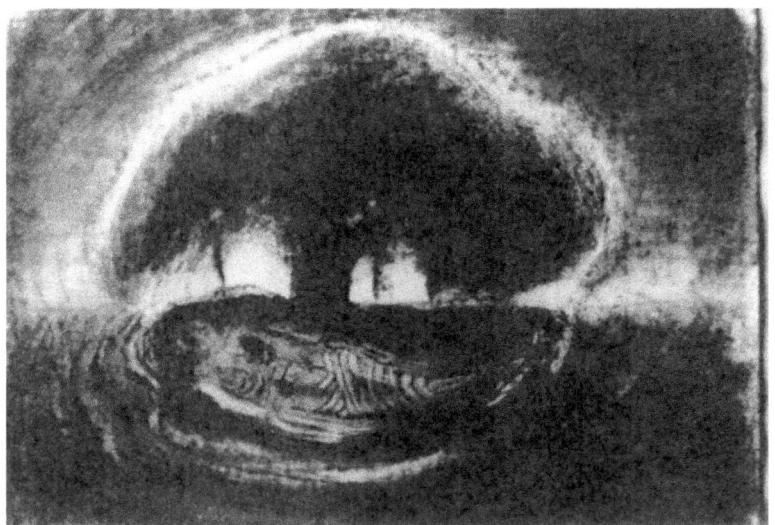

Catherine Arthur, 'Boudicca', 1991, from 'The Cancer Drawings of Catherine Arthur' by Amanda Sebestyen, *Feminist Review*, No. 41 (Summer 1992), p. 36.

In the twentieth and twenty-first centuries, women's appropriations of Boudicca have taken many forms and, unlike the satirical jibes at Thatcher by male adversaries and commentators, have overwhelmingly tended to treat her with respect and admiration. In one particularly personal appropriation, artist Catherine Arthur created a series of drawings chronicling her battle with breast cancer, including one entitled 'Boudicca'. The image represents Arthur's interpretation of death and depicts Boudicca buried beneath a mushroom-shaped tree, which, according to Amanda Sebestyen is also 'a placenta, nourishing her [Boudicca] as a foetus waiting under the earth'.[20] The skeletal Boudicca is missing her left breast, which is perhaps an allusion to the alleged meaning of the word 'Amazon', namely 'without a breast', and the accompanying tradition associating Boudicca with this legendary tribe of warrior women. More specifically, however, it is a statement on the artist's own body as it suffered the ravages of breast cancer. The hole where the breast should be is filled with a blossoming rose, a sign of life from what remains of the body. Sebestyen also explains that 'incidentally, Boadicea is supposed to have been buried on Parliament Hill, around the corner from that North London house where the Cancer Drawings … were made'. Feminist artists, like Arthur, who record their journey towards death are not only brave but artistically, morally and perhaps spiritually triumphant – not because they win the battle – but because they do not. Arthur's choice of Boudicca to symbolise her own plight further articulates this paradigm by eliding her own ill-fated war against breast cancer with Boudicca's similarly doomed campaign against the Romans.

In a footnote to Arthur's medical battle, Cancer Research UK's Race for Life 2008 utilised a well-known statue of Boudicca, along with other public images of historical women including Jane Austen (Bath) and Emmeline Pankhurst (Westminster, London) to promote a charity fundraising event series. A women's-only event, the Race for Life sees women walking, jogging and running five kilometres (3.1 miles) at approximately three hundred locations across Britain. In keeping with the theme, the statue of Boudicca and her daughters by J. Havard Thomas (1916) that adorns the first floor landing of City Hall, Cardiff wore a white running vest with a pink insert advertising Race for Life 2008. In press releases for the event, the organisation explained that they chose public images of women who are renowned for their strength and historical significance. In this instance, the public and political images of women such as Boudicca and Pankhurst are reinforced and reinvented in a way that speaks to modern women and the life-threatening problems that confront them in the contemporary West.

That Boudicca still resonates in the lives of modern English women in particular, is attested in the poetry of Jane Holland who has also personalised Boudicca in the collection entitled *Boudicca &*

Cancer Research UK's Race for Life 2008 advertisement
utilising 'Boadicea' by J. Havard Thomas (1916).

Co (2006).[21] In the final section of this four-part collection, Holland
has written the series simply called 'Boudicca', in which she traces the
chronology of the leader's life, from birth ('Red Star') to death
('Suicide'). Holland's claim to the historical icon has resulted in
fictional poems, such as 'Boudicca's Son', to personal interpretations
of Boudicca's encounters with the Romans, which comprise the

majority of the pieces. Boudicca's relationship with her husband is also dealt with, including one of Holland's most powerful poems in the collection, 'Not Exactly a Virgin':

> I married Prasutagus in the spring.
> We did it the old-fashioned way –
> slaughtered everything
> and feasted till May.
>
> I remember blossom falling.
> He was the stag
> and I was the hind
> running wild before him.
>
> Prasutagus was a good man
> and a better king. I let him
> catch me, push me
> to the earth, laughing.
>
> There was no pain that day
> or in what followed.
> In those days, I was less fussy
> what I put in my mouth.
>
> I wasn't exactly a virgin
> but I hadn't yet seen
> a woman's throat ripped out
> for refusing to swallow.

The power inherent in 'Not Exactly a Virgin' results from the poet's ability to combine a private voice enhanced by the use of the personal pronoun 'I' with the historical, and thereby public, image of Boudicca as the ravaged woman of Roman conquest. Boudicca's narrative is characterised by a combination of recollections of her youth – symbolised by the moment of loss of virginity

– and her present condition as one of colonialism's wounded indigenes. This dual poetic voice is preoccupied with self-representation based on the body, its gender and its sexuality. As Tacitus writes of Boudicca's body damaged and the bodies of her daughters despoiled, Holland creates a Boudicca who meditates on her present status through her body; there is the delight of a young woman's first experiences with sexual pleasure, and there is the use of the female body as the site of masculine power in its most base expression.

The Boudicca of Holland also finds her self-expression through the evocation of the land to which she is so inextricably tied. In 'Not Exactly a Virgin', Boudicca speaks of the season of spring, of the stag and the hind, and of the earth on which she lies with Prasutagus. Likewise, in the closing poem of the collection, 'Suicide', she speaks of 'British dirt', symbolic of the very ground from which she was birthed:

> In the end, they had to use a crowbar
> on my teeth, to force the poison in.
>
> They didn't even bother raping me.
>
> After the first breath, I was high
> on mercury, lungs pure silver.
>
> I was radioactive: they could have
> found me in the dark. How Suetonius,
> that fat Roman dumpling,
> must have laughed. The end
> was confused. Some screaming, vomit.
> It hurt, I know that much.
>
> Nothing else. Just good British dirt
> and closing my mouth on it.

Here she recalls the sentiments of 'Not Exactly a Virgin' in her reflections on the female mouth as the signifier of masculine imperialism. The physical embodiment of a woman's sexuality – as well as her voice – the mouth operates for Holland's Boudicca as a symbol of focus for patriarchal authority; silencing it, raping it, poisoning it. Yet Holland's Boudicca is also an anti-hero, a construct partially ensconced in the poet's determination not to have her become a perpetual victim. Thus, with the complexity of Tacitus' warrior, Holland's persona is also complicit in savagery, best illustrated in 'Headless Woman':

> They were never expecting us.
>
> Gates were always wide open.
> We ate Romans for breakfast
> and raped the livestock.
> It all got mildly out of hand
> after Camulodunum.
> Kids murdered, mass graves
> stinking behind villas.
>
> Once, I slipped on a brain
> in the road: decapitated owner
> half-lying, half-sitting
> against the ruins of her house.
>
> I couldn't help laughing;
> she looked so comical,
> feet dragged in the dirt,
> spare head grinning.

Boudicca's casual attitude towards the ferocity of the rebels – including her own outrageous acts – is not only defiant but unsettling. As she speaks of her own connections to the land, be it the dirt of

'Suicide' or the more gentle 'earth' of 'Not Exactly a Virgin', here she is disdainful of 'feet dragged in the dirt' as she mocks the decapitated woman amid 'the ruins of her house.'

Conclusion

The power of Jane Holland's poetry attests to the power of her subject matter, which in turn becomes another page in the fictional tradition stretching back over two thousand years. When one reads Tacitus and Dio on Boudicca, she becomes as real as any historical personage – as real as Julius Caesar or Claudius, the emperors whose reigns oversaw the beginning of the end for the Iceni and set the groundwork for the definitive Roman conquest of Britain. Yet when one stops reading and begins to actually contemplate what has been read, these versions of Boudicca seem to be ephemeral creations that shine brightly, excitedly, but then quickly fade as doubt begins to settle in. Perhaps it is because of this effect, the effect of a seductively real heroine, who remains within the pages once the book has closed, that she has become such a popular topic for historical fiction; be it Rosemary Sutcliff's children's account, *Song for a Dark Queen*, or Manda Scott's adult series. When one reads the work of such writers, the experience is not far removed from the process of reading Tacitus and Dio.

What is more important than assessing how accurate the existing 'evidence' may be, though, is an appreciation of how important the icon has become. Boudicca was crafted by Tacitus, then Dio, in order to communicate specific ideals, messages and morals. Likewise, when one examines subsequent treatments of her, the quest is to find and appreciate the personal meanings contained therein. These personal meanings can be as specific and private as Catherine Arthur's

'Boudicca' from her cancer series or as collectively exclusive as the British elevation of her to a national or imperial emblem.

So ingrained is Boudicca within the English psyche that it is hardly surprising to discover that she is believed to haunt certain parts of the country; Lincolnshire and Essex are among the regions where there have been alleged sightings of Boudicca's ghost. While records of such encounters are scant, the existence of the reports, some spanning over a hundred years, has rendered Boudicca a source of urban myth and legend. People search for her burial site and as a result there are further myths and legends concerning where she rests, including arguably the most common and persistent claim: under Platforms 8, 9 or 10 of King's Cross Station. In 2006, however, *The Sun* newspaper ran a somewhat hysterical article claiming that Boudicca's last stand – ergo, her resting place – might well be at the Birmingham suburb of Kings Norton, right next to another successful empire, McDonald's.

These stories keep Boudicca alive in a very different way to her written and artistic receptions, revealing a need for some to 'see' her in the form of an apparition, or to be able to 'point' to where she lies. To the ghost hunters and the tomb searchers, Boudicca remains a shadowy figure, but she does so for all of us; an elusive, ultimately imaginary icon.

Notes

Introduction

1. Sandra R. Joshel, 'Female Desire and the Discourse of Empire: Tacitus' Messalina', *Signs* 21 (1995), 50-82 at 52.

1. Boudicca and the British Revolt Against Rome

1. The word 'Celt' in many ways reflects the idea of an 'imagined community', a concept developed by Benedict Anderson in *Imagined Communities: Reflections on the Origin and Spread of Nationalism* (1983; London: Verso: 1991).

2. On the height of the Britons, see Strabo *Geography* 4.5.3 and Tacitus *Agricola* 11. Interestingly, however, excavations that have unearthed skeletal remains from the era rarely support this physical characteristic (Vanessa Collingridge 195). On the use of the Greek word *megiste*, which, as noted in the text is usually rendered 'tall', a more accurate translation would be 'large', as adopted in my translation in Chapter 3.

3. See Callimachus (c. 310-240 BC) 'Hymn to Delos' 173-4 where the Celts are referred to as 'Titans of a later day'.

4. The translation of Strabo is by Horace Leonard Jones, *Strabo: Geography Books 3-5* (Cambridge, MA: Harvard University Press, 1923).

5. For a concise survey on relations between Augustus and the Britons, see Miranda Aldhouse-Green, 11-13. See also Strabo: 'At present, however, some of the chieftains there, having gained the friendship of Caesar Augustus through embassies and paying court to him, have set up votive offerings on the Capitolium and have almost made the whole island Roman property. In addition they submit so readily to heavy duties both on the exports from there to Gaul and on the imports from Gaul' (translation by S. Ireland, 37).

6. As P.A. Brunt and J.M. Moore (*Res Gestae Divi Augusti*, Oxford: Oxford University Press, 1970) note: 'Strabo's *embassies* must surely be distinct from the

arrival of *refugee* princes at Augustus' court' (74). Dumnobellanus is named and generally assumed to be the same Dumnobellanus whose coins have been found in Britain. The second name has been damaged, with only the first three letters, 'Tim...', extant; from coins discovered in 1996, the name Tincomarus is the reconstruction, which reveals his identity as the leader of the Atrebates from southern central Britain. On the latter, see John Creighton, *Coins and Power in Late Iron Age Britain* (Cambridge: Cambridge University Press, 2000), 117-18.

7. On the theories as to what Caligula was actually doing near Boulogne during the early months of AD 40, see David Woods, 'Caligula's Seashells', *Greece & Rome* 47 (2000), 80-7; see also Anthony A. Barrett, *Caligula: The Corruption of Power* (New Haven: Yale University Press, 1998), 136-7.

8. Dio names him 'Berikos' (*Ep.* 60.19) but Celtic coins clarify the name as 'Verica' (Guy de la Bédoyère, 23).

9. On the numismatic and archaeological evidence, see A.A. Barrett, 'Claudius' British Victory Arch in Rome', *Britannia* 22 (2000), 1-19.

10. Despite no mention of his name in any of the extant written sources, coinage from Iceni hoards attest to the likelihood that Antedios was king of the tribe at the time of the invasion of AD 43; see D.F. Allen; see also Paul R. Sealey, 5 and Christopher Allen Snyder, 35.

11. On the list of the twenty ancient sources on the Druids, composed between the fourth century BC and the fourth century AD, see Jane Webster, 'At the End of the World: Druidic and Other Revitalization Movements in Post-Conquest Gaul and Britain', *Britannia* 30 (1999), 1-20.

12. Watling Street is the name of the track that extends, east to west, across Britain; it has two starting points – Dover and Richborough (both on the coast of Kent) – and from either locale it travels north-east to London (Londinium) via St Albans (Verulamium), then to High Cross (Venonis) and Wroxeter (Virconium); it crosses the river Severn and then, turning south, ends at Leintwardine (Bravonium).

13. See Ralph Merrifield, *London, City of the Romans* (Berkeley: University of California Press, 1983), 42.

14. See Barry C. Burnham, 'Celts and Romans: Towards a Romano-Celtic Society', in *The Celtic World*, ed. Green, 121-41; Burnham provides an extensive list of Jones' work on agriculture.

15. It is estimated that there are around 15,000 coins from the territory of the Iceni; see Richard Hingley and Christina Unwin (27).

2. Tacitus' Account

1. G.B. Townend does not support Cluvius Rufus as a major source for Tacitus but argues for Pliny the Elder, see Townend 470-1.

2. Around AD 106 or 107, Tacitus wrote to Pliny the Younger, asking for an account of Pliny the Elder's death in the eruption of Mt. Vesuvius (*Epistle* 6.16). Pliny replied with an extensive narrative, to which Tacitus responded requesting further details, thus prompting a second letter (*Epistle* 6.20).

3. On human sacrifice among the so-called barbaric peoples of antiquity, see J. Rives, 'Human Sacrifice among Pagans and Christians', *Journal of Roman Studies* 85 (1995), 65-85; A.M. Eckstein, 'Human Sacrifice and Fear of Military Disaster in Republican Rome', *American Journal of Ancient History* 7 (1982), 69-75. Rives includes a discussion of allegations of human sacrifice performed by the Romans (prior to the late republic); see, for example, p. 84 on Plutarch's views on the sacrifice of two Greeks and two Gauls during the Second Punic War.

4. C.J. Simpson argues that in this instance, Tacitus is using the story preserved in Zonaras 8.1, which tells of a statue of Victory in the Roman forum that mysteriously fell, turning to face the enemy, prior to the battle of Sentinum in 295 BC. The problem, however, is the source for this twelfth-century Byzantine chronicler; if it were Dio, for example, as T.P. Wiseman (119) suggests, Simpson's argument becomes problematic (possibly both Tacitus and Zonaras were utilising a local legend concerning the statue). See Wiseman, *Remus: A Roman Myth* (Cambridge: Cambridge University Press, 1995). See also Giles Standing, 373-5.

5. Tacitus does not outline the role of Catus Decianus in the cause of the rebellion, but assumes his readers are aware of the events; Dio specifies that the procurator (*Ep.* 62.2) had earned the hatred of the Britons through enforcing repayment of monies provided by Claudius to leading men. On Catus' departure to Gaul, see Graham Webster, 91.

6. See G.I.A.D. Draper, 'The Origins of the Just War Traditions', in *Reflections on Law and Armed Conflicts: The Selected Works on the Laws of War by the late Professor Colonel G.I.A.D. Draper, OBE*, ed. M.A. Meyer and H. McCoubrey (The Hague: Kluwer Law International, 1964; 1999), 5-9. Draper discusses what he interprets to be the decline in Roman adherence to this concept in the era of the empire:

It must be admitted that the place of the 'just and pious war' was in decline by the later Republican epoch. However, it may be said that in relation to the time of the late Roman Empire the practices of warfare in Republican times were comparatively moderate and restrained. The tragedy of Roman civilization was the departure from the values of Republican society in favour of the grossly depraved and evil way of life that emerged under Empire (6).

7. See Tacitus' *Agricola* 31 where reference to the Romans defiling Celtic women is 'put into the mouth' of Calgacus.

8. Venutius was clearly referred to in one of the lost books of the *Annals*.

9. See Introduction, n. 1 at 60.

10. The years of Claudius' reign from AD 37 to 48 are, unfortunately, part of the missing books of the *Annals*.

11. Decimus Valerius Asiaticus (d. AD 47) was twice consul (AD 35 and 46) and husband of Lollia Saturnia, the sister of Caligula's third wife, Lollia Paulina.

12. Anthony A. Barrett, *Agrippina: Sex, Power and Politics in the Early Empire* (London: Routledge, 1999).

3. Dio Cassius' Account

1. Ronald Mellor, *The Historians of Ancient Rome*, 2nd edn (London: Routledge, 2004). For an account of Dio's public career, see Martin Hose, 'Cassius Dio: A Senator and Historian in the Age of Anxiety', in *A Companion to Greek and Roman Historiography*, ed. John Marincola (Oxford: Blackwell, 2008), 462.

2. E. Schwartz, 'Cassius Dio', *Realencyklopädie für protestantische Theologie und Kirche* 3 (1899) 1684-722; Fergus Millar, *A Study of Dio Cassius* (Oxford: Clarendon Press, 1964), 148-50.

3. Christoph M. Bulst (496 n. 3) notes the sources other than Dio 62.7 for the suddenness of the uprising, citing Tac. *Agr.* 16, *Ann.* 14.30 and 32.4.

4. Christopher Pelling, 'Biographical History? Cassius Dio on the Early Principate', in *Portraits: Biographical Representation in the Greek and Latin Literature of the Roman Empire*, ed. Mark J. Edwards and Simon Swain (Oxford: Oxford University Press, 1997), 117-44.

5. For an excellent discussion of the gaze of the ancient statue, see Deborah Tarn Steiner, *Images in Mind: Statues in Archaic and Classical Greek Literature and Thought* (Princeton: Princeton University Press, 2002) 156-84.

6. Collingridge takes Dio's reference to the torc at face value, providing supporting archaeological evidence: 'torcs have been found in burial hoards including the remarkable Snettisham hoards which contained a variety of styles, sizes and dates of deposit, from the mid-first century BC to the first century AD' (196). See also Aldhouse-Green (27).

7. Male-male erotic acts were regularly cited in vituperative texts, yet Boudicca's reference extends the insult by stating that the males the Romans engaged with sexually included youths 'past their prime' (*Ep.* 62.6.4), suggesting that they were of citizen age and therefore, in the traditional Roman value system, particularly out of bounds. To engage sexually with youths of citizen class was for the Romans a taboo in itself, but to have contact with a youth who has received the *toga virilis* (the toga of manhood, granted at the age of fourteen), was a violation. Slaves were a different matter, but as Boudicca regards all Roman men as slaves, the potential distinction between citizen boys and slave boys cleverly disintegrates.

8. Rankin suggests that the act of cutting off the breasts of the women 'probably indicates an intrinsic cruelty in the cult of the Celtic goddess of war – here the relevant deity is probably a goddess called Andrasta or Andarta' (1996: 222).

9. G. Fincham, 'Writing Colonial Conflict, Acknowledging Colonial Weakness', *TRAC 2000: Proceedings of the Tenth Annual Theoretical Roman Archaeology Conference, London 2004*, ed. G. Davies, A. Gardner and K. Lockyear (Oxford: Oxbow, 2001), 25-34.

10. *virtus*: manly valour; the essence of manliness or masculinity; *mos maiorum*: the traditions and the actions of the ancestors or forefathers.

11. P.A. Brunt, 'Reflections on British and Roman Imperialism', *Comparative Studies in Society and History* 7 (1965), 267-88. On the influence of Thucydides on Dio, see Hose (n. 1 above).

12. The translation of Thucydides is by Thomas Hobbes, *The English Works of Thomas Hobbes of Malmesbury; Now First Collected and Edited by Sir William Molesworth, Bart.*, vol. 8 (London: Bohn, 1839).

13. Clifford Orwin, *The Humanity of Thucydides* (Princeton: Princeton University Press, 1994).

4. After the Ancients: Boudicca's Later Lives

1. The translation of Gildas is by J.A. Giles, *Six Old English Chronicles* (London: H.G. Bohn, 1848).

2. E.A. Thompson, 'Gildas and the History of Britain', *Britannia* 10 (1979), 203-26.

3. Sharon Macdonald's (47) rendering of Bellenden's 1551 translation.

4. Carolyn D. Williams notes the discrepancy in the historical accounts of the delivery of the speech: 'according to one account, she made a speech directly to her army; another version of the story says she gave a message privately to the sergeant major, asking him to deliver it to the troops after she had gone. In the first case, there are possible echoes of Boudicca in the speech; in the second, the echoes are much fainter, but an

explicit comparison is made between the two queens' (192). For a version of the speech, see *The Norton Anthology of English Literature*, 6th edn, vol. 1, ed. M.H. Abrams (New York: W.W. Norton & Company, 1993), 999. For further discussion of the authenticity of the actual words, see Williams, 192-3 (perhaps Elizabeth I, like Boudicca, had her words, her sentiments, literally man-handled as well).

5. On the other (front) side of the statue is this inscription:

BOADICEA
BOUDICCA
QUEEN OF THE ICENI
WHO DIED IN AD 61
AFTER LEADING HER PEOPLE
AGAINST THE ROMAN INVADER

6. Written in galliambics, as used by the Latin poet Catullus (*c.* 84-*c.* 54 BC) in Poem 63 on the mythical figure of Attis, Tennyson's 'Boadicea' is difficult to read from a metrical point of view. 'Tennyson admitted the metrical unintelligibility of his own Boadicea – "who can read her except myself?" ' (Robert Cummings, 'Tennyson, Trench, Tholuck and the "Oriental" Metre of "Locksley Hall" ', *Translation and Literature* 1 [1992], 130; from a letter to the Duke of Argyll).

7. Examples of male artists include: Matt Hughes' 'Death of the Iceni Queen' (2005); Howard David Johnson's 'Warrior Queen Boudica' (2005); Jedediah Dougherty (2006); Mike Penn, 'Boudica' (2008). Dougherty's image is not of a sex-goddess or delectable victim, but a grotesque Amazon, amply bosomed (of course), but not primarily there to entice the male gaze.

8. Judy Chicago, *Embroidering our Heritage: The Dinner Party Needlework* (New York: Doubleday, 1980).

9. Judy Grahn, *Another Mother Tongue: Gay Words, Gay Worlds* (Boston: Beacon Press, 1984).

10. Banksy, *Wall and Piece* (London: Century, 2005), 208.

11. Dora Montefiore, *From a Victorian to a Modern* (London: E. Archer, 1927), 109.

12. Sylvia Pankhurst, *The Suffragette: The History of the Women's Militant Suffrage Movement* (1911; London: Read Books, 2009), 72.

13. Paula Bartley, *Emmeline Pankhurst* (London: Routlege, 2002), 123.

14. Hilda Kean, 'Public History and Popular Memory: Issues in the Commemoration of the British Militant Suffrage Campaign', *Women's History Review* 14 (2005), 581-602, at 582.

15. Miles Franklin, *A Gregarious Culture: Topical Writings of Miles Franklin*, ed. Jill Roe and Margaret Bettison (Queensland: University of Queensland Press, 2001), 51.

Franklin is commenting on Pankhurst's visit to the United States; the article first appeared as 'Mrs Pankhurst in the United States', in *Life and Labor*, Dec. 1913: 364-6 (under the initials S.M.F.).

16. Mary Phillips, 'A Typical Suffragette', *Votes for Women*, December 1907, 35, quoted in Bartley, 108.

17. Quoted in *Feminism and the Periodical Press, 1900-1918,* vol. 3, ed. Lucy Delap, Maria DiCenzo and Leila Ryan (London: Routledge, 2006).

18. Elizabeth Somerville (Bessie Watson), interviewed by Helen Clark in 1986; 'The People's Story, Edinburgh Museums and Galleries'. According to Clark, attempts to track down the brooch have been unsuccessful.

19. Quoted in Leslie Banker and William Mullins, *Britannia in Brief: The Scoop on All Things British* (London: Ballantine Books, 2009), 7.

20. Amanda Sebestyen, 'The Cancer Drawings of Catherine Arthur', *Feminist Review* 41 (Summer, 1992): 27-36, at 35.

21. Jane Holland, *Boudicca & Co.* (Cambridge: Salt, 2006).

Select Bibliography

Adler, Eric (2008) 'Boudica's Speeches in Tacitus and Dio', *Classical World* 101: 173-95.

Aldhouse-Green, Miranda (2006) *Boudica Britannia* (Great Britain: Pearson Education Ltd).

Allen, D.F. (1970) 'The Coins of the Iceni', *Britannia* 1: 1-33.

Bédoyère, Guy de la (2006) *Roman Britain: A New History* (London: Thames & Hudson).

Black, E.W. (2001) 'The First Century Historians of Roman Britain', *Oxford Journal of Archaeology* 20: 415-28.

Braund, David (1996) *Ruling Roman Britain: Kings, Queens, Governors and Emperors from Julius Caesar to Agricola* (London: Routledge).

Bulst, Christoph M. (1961), 'The Revolt of Queen Boudicca in AD 60', *Historia: Zeitschrift für Alte Geschichte* 10: 496-509.

Burnham, Barry C. (1995) 'Celts and Romans: Towards a Romano-Celtic Society', in Miranda J. Green (ed.) *The Celtic World* (London: Routledge) 121-41.

Carr, Gillian (2005) 'Woad, Tattooing and Identity in Later Iron Age and Early Roman Britain', *Oxford Journal of Archaeology* 24: 273-92.

Collingridge, Vanessa (2006) *Boudica* (Berkshire: Ebury Press).

Collingwood, R.G. and J.N.L. Myres (1937) *Roman Britain and the English Settlements*, 2nd edn (Oxford: Clarendon Press).

Creighton, John (1995) 'Visions of Power: Imagery and Symbols in Late Iron Age Britain', *Britannia* 26: 285-301.

Davies, John (2008) *The Land of Boudica: Prehistoric and Roman Norfolk* (Oxford: Oxbow Books).

Dyson, Stephen L. (1971) 'Native Revolts in the Roman Empire', *Historia: Zeitschrift für Alte Geschichte* 20: 239-74.

Eckstein, Arthur M. (1982) 'Human Sacrifice and Fear of Military Disaster in Republican Rome', *American Journal of Ancient History* 7 (1982): 69-75.

149

Ellis, Peter Berresford (2002) *A Brief History of the Druids* (UK: Running Press).

Evans, Christopher (2003) 'Britons and Romans at Chatteris: Investigations at Langwood Farm, Cambridgeshire', *Britannia* 34: 175-264.

Fraser, Antonia (1988) *Boudicea's Chariot: The Warrior Queens* (London: Weidenfeld & Nicolson).

Frénée-Hutchins, Samantha (2009) 'The Cultural and Ideological Significance of Representations of Boudica During the Reigns of Elizabeth I and James I', PhD diss. (Exeter University and Université D'Orléans).

Frere, Sheppard (1987) *Britannia: A History of Roman Britain* (London: Routledge & Kegan Paul).

Gowing, Alain M. (1997) 'Cassius Dio on the Reign of Nero', *Aufstieg und Niedergang der römischen Welt* 2.34.3: 2558-90.

Green, Miranda J. (ed.) (1995) *The Celtic World* (London: Routledge).

Hingley, Richard and Christina Unwin (2005) *Boudica: Iron Age Warrior Queen* (London: Hambledon Continuum).

Howarth, Nicki (2008) *Cartimandua: Queen of the Brigantes* (Gloucestershire: The History Press).

Ireland, S. (1996) *Roman Britain: A Sourcebook*, 2nd edn (London: Routledge).

Johns, Catherine (1996) *The Jewellery of Roman Britain: Celtic and Classical Traditions* (London: Routledge).

Keegan, Peter (2004) 'Boudica, Cartimandua, Messalina and Agrippina the Younger. Independent Women of Power and the Gendered Rhetoric of Roman History', *Ancient History* 34: 99-148.

Levene, D.S. (2009) 'Speeches in the *Histories*', in A.J. Woodman (ed.) *The Cambridge Companion to Tacitus* (Cambridge: Cambridge University Press): 212-24.

Macdonald, Sharon (1987) 'Boadicea: Warrior, Mother and Myth', in Pat Holden Macdonald and Shirley Ardner (eds) *Images of Women in Peace and War* (London: Macmillan Education) 40-61.

Marincola, John (1997) *Authority and Tradition in Ancient Historiography* (Cambridge: Cambridge University Press).

Mattingly, David (2006) *An Imperial Possession: Britain in the Roman Empire* (Great Britain: Allen Lane).

Mikalachki, Jodi (1998) *The Legacy of Boadicea: Gender and Nation in Early Modern England* (London: Routledge).

Millar, Fergus (1964) *A Study of Cassius Dio* (Oxford: Clarendon Press).

Miller, N.P. (1964) 'Dramatic Speech in Tacitus', *American Journal of Philology* 85: 279-96.

Select Bibliography

Overbeck, John C. (1969) 'Tacitus and Dio on Boudicca's Rebellion', *American Journal of Philology* 90: 129-45.

Potter, T.W. (1983) *Roman Britain* (Cambridge, MA: Harvard University Press).

Rankin, David (1995) 'The Celts Through Classical Eyes', in Miranda J. Green (ed.) *The Celtic World* (London: Routledge) 21-36.

Rankin, David (1996) *Celts and the Classical World*, 2nd edn (London: Routledge).

Richmond, I.A. (1954) 'Queen Cartimandua', *Journal of Roman Studies* 44: 43-52.

Santoro L'hoir, Francesca (1994) 'Tacitus and Women's Usurpation of Power', *Classical World* 88: 5-26.

Sealey, Paul R. (1997) *The Boudican Revolt Against Rome* (Buckinghamshire: Shire Archaeology).

Simpson, C.J. (1996) 'The Statue of Victory at Colchester', *Britannia* 27: 386-7.

Snyder, Christopher Allen (2003) *The Britons* (London: Wiley-Blackwell).

Spence, Lewis (1937) *Boadicea, Warrior Queen of the Britons* (London: Robert Hale).

Standing, Giles (2005) 'The Varain Disaster and the Boudiccan Revolt: Fabled Victories?', *Britannia* 36: 373-5.

Stewart, P.C.N. (1995) 'Inventing Britain: The Roman Creation and Adaptation of an Image', *Britannia* 26: 1-10.

Todd, Malcolm (1999) *Roman Britain* 3rd edn (London: Blackwell).

Townend, G.B. (1964) 'Some Rhetorical Battle-Pictures in Dio', *Hermes* 92: 467-81.

Trow, M.J. (1964) 'Cluvius Rufus in the *Histories* of Tacitus', *American Journal of Philology* 85: 337-77.

Trow, M.J. (2003) *Boudicca: The Warrior Queen* (United Kingdom: Sutton Publishing).

Wacher, John (1997) *The Towns of Roman Britain*, 2nd edn (London: Routledge).

Webster, Graham (1993) *Boudica: The British Revolt Against Rome AD 60*, rev. edn (London: Routledge).

Williams, Carolyn D. (2009) *Boudica and Her Stories: Narrative Transformations of a Warrior Queen* (Newark: University of Delaware Press).

Index